no-fuss **dinners**

no-fuss dinners

deliciously simple recipes for cooking after work

Caroline Marson photography by Peter Cassidy

RYLAND
PETERS
& SMALL

LONDON NEW YORK

Dedication

For Simon, Freddie, and Daisy…

First published in the USA in 2006
by Ryland Peters & Small, Inc.
519 Broadway, 5th Floor
New York NY 10012
www.rylandpeters.com

10 9 8 7 6 5 4 3 2 1

Text © Caroline Marson 2006
Design and photographs
© Ryland Peters & Small 2006

Library of Congress Cataloging-in-Publication Data
Marson, Caroline.
  No-fuss dinners / Caroline Marson ; photography by
Peter Cassidy. -- 1st ed.
    p. cm.
  Includes index.
  ISBN-13: 978-1-84597-212-7
  ISBN-10: 1-84597-212-0
  1. Dinners and dining. 2. Quick and easy cookery. I.
Title.
  TX737.M3785 2006
  641.5'55--dc22
                                          2006011064

Design and photographic art direction Steve Painter
Commissioning Editor Julia Charles
Production Gordana Simakovic
Art Director Anne-Marie Bulat
Publishing Director Alison Starling

Food Stylist Tonia George
Prop Stylist Liz Belton
Indexer Hilary Bird

Notes
• All spoon measurements are level unless
otherwise stated.
• Eggs are large unless otherwise specified. Uncooked
or partially cooked eggs should not be served to the
very old, frail, young children, pregnant women, or
those with compromised immune systems.

Author's acknowledgements
Thanks goes to my wise mother who was a spot-on guinea pig
and put up with her kitchen being wrecked for a week. Thanks
to my father for his creative thinking and encouragement.
Thanks also to my lovely husband Simon who spent ages
gazing into the fridge wondering what combination he was
allowed to eat and what he had to keep his hands off! Thanks to
my son Freddie for continuously making me laugh and for
creating delightful concoctions in a vain hope that they might
make the book. A huge thank you also goes to all at Ryland
Peters & Small—especially Alison Starling, Julia Charles, and
Steve Painter—and to photographer Pete Cassidy and food
stylist Tonia George. And finally, a big thank you to all my
girlfriends who helped me with the school run, entertained my
son, and walked my dog Daisy.

contents

introduction

This book is for busy people with hectic lives who enjoy good food but have little or no time to cook. Whether you have a long commute to and from work each day, or juggle school runs with part-time work, the chances are you live your life in the fast lane. Perhaps understandably, taking time to cook a fresh meal from scratch is often low on the list of priorities. Frozen entrées, processed foods, and carryouts seem like a good solution for the time-poor, but they are not the answer. They are often high in salt, fat, and artificial additives and low in taste. And, quite simply, there is no pleasure to be had from putting a packaged meal in the microwave—it is a short-term fix with no heart or soul. Cooking is a pleasurable and therapeutic pastime and the ideal way to unwind after a long and demanding day.

In *No-fuss Dinners* I will show you how to make the most of good, fresh ingredients and help you understand that, by keeping things simple, it's possible to look forward to an imaginative evening meal without dreading the cooking during the day. I use ingredients that are available in most supermarkets and have made the methods of cooking as short and straightforward as possible. The recipes are all suitable for beginners and more experienced cooks alike, and include No-cook Deli Dinners (imaginative ideas for quickly assembled pizzas, pastas, and platters), Simple Dishes for every day, Light Bites for when soup or a salad is all you fancy, Dinner for Friends for slightly more sophisticated evenings, and a selection of delicious treats in Sweet Things. Finally, in Transforming Simple Food I show you how creative use of pestos, butters, marinades, rubs, and dressings can turn a simple meal into something really special.

All of these recipes should not take longer than 30 minutes to prepare from start to finish and some take even less time or need no cooking at all. Most of the recipes serve two people because that's how many of us live these days, but halve or double up as you need to. Make sure you have a good array of different sized, heavy-based pots and pans. Additionally, good-quality knives, kept razor sharp and safely put away in a knife block, are a must.

Easy steps to No-fuss Dinners:

★ Begin by planning for when you are likely to be in or out during the weeks ahead and shop accordingly. This common-sense approach will mean you can buy foods specifically for each night rather than randomly buying foods that will not be used. Make a list and stick to it—don't be tempted to impulse buy.

★ Shop weekly for fresh fruit and vegetables or use an organic box delivery service. Choose seasonal foods when possible as they will last longer and taste better.

★ Become a regular at your local gourmet shop or supermarket deli counter and buy semi-prepared ingredients for quick dinners.

★ Stock up on pantry essentials such as spices, sauces, and flavorings and use them to add depth and flavor to basic foods (see pages 8–9).

★ Fill your freezer with bags of convenient frozen fresh foods such as vegetables, fish and seafood, mixed berries, and packages of chopped fresh herbs (see page 9). Double up when cooking and freeze extra servings to enjoy on another evening. Make sure you always have plenty of freezer bags and freezer-proof airtight plastic containers on hand.

★ Prepare ahead—many dishes can be part-assembled in the morning or even the night before and stored in the fridge until needed. Also, if you are chopping onions or garlic for today's supper, chop a little extra for tomorrow. These ingredients will stay fresh in the fridge for up to 4 days if stored in sealed containers.

I hope you will be inspired by these simple recipes. The ingredients and methods suggested are not cast in stone; they are flexible and designed to encourage you to be creative, so do experiment and tweak them to suit your own taste as you go along. Discover your own favorites and wave goodbye to processed meals once and for all!

pantry essentials

It's a good idea to keep your pantry, fridge, and freezer well stocked with useful ingredients—you'll always be able to produce a quick dinner, even if you've not had time to buy anything in. Any additional fresh food should be bought often and in small quantities so that it is always the freshest it can be.

Staples
You will never be far from a meal if you have these key staple ingredients ready and waiting in your kitchen cupboards.

★ **Dried pasta**—make sure it says durum wheat or semolina pasta. Keep a good selection of pasta shapes in your pantry, from penne or rigatoni to spaghetti or tagliatelle.
★ **Rice**—long grain, basmati, Thai jasmine or fragrant, and microwavable rice; Arborio for risottos.
★ **Egg or rice noodles**—look for "straight-to-wok" brands for stir-fries.
★ **Couscous**—great for spicy dishes. Just needs plumping up in hot water or stock.
★ **Pizza crusts**—either long-life or frozen.
★ **Beans**—cans of cooked, mixed beans, including kidney, cannellini, and butter beans, and chickpeas.
★ **Canned chopped tomatoes**—either plain or seasoned with mixed herbs or garlic. Great for instant pizza base sauce.
★ **Tuna flakes**—canned or in jars with olive oil for salads.
★ **Crab meat**—cans of crab meat are handy for making fishcakes and adding to salads.
★ **Coconut milk**—for Thai curries and soups.
★ **Toasted nuts**—pine nuts, almonds, hazelnuts etc., stored in airtight containers.
★ **Pumpkin and sunflower seeds**—useful for snacking and sprinkling on salads.
★ **Black and green olives**—keep jars of olives, either plain or marinated.
★ **Capers**—jars of small capers and large caperberries for pasta, pizza, and fish dishes.
★ **Porridge oats**—for making flapjacks and desserts. Choose old-fashioned rolled oats.

Flavor enhancers
Add these seasonings only after you have tasted the food. A pinch or a drop will add "high" or "low" tones to your cooking.

★ **Sea salt flakes** and **freshly ground black pepper**—essential seasoning.
★ **Dark and light soy sauce**—for adding salt to Asian dishes.
★ **Thai fish sauce (nam pla)**—add to all Thai food for that instant authentic flavor.
★ **Lemon and lime juice**—use instead of salt for adding "high" tones.
★ **Balsamic vinegar**—syrupy balsamic vinegar. Put in a spray bottle and spritz onto salads.
★ **Vinegars**—cider, white wine, red wine, and tarragon for dressings.
★ **Mustards**—Dijon—smooth or grainy—and English mustard.
★ **Anchovy paste or fillets**—this paste has a long fridge life. Great for adding flavor.
★ **Tomato paste**—adds depth to tomato sauces.
★ **Pomegranate molasses**—a thick, sweet syrup good for dressings.

Oils
Using the right oil can make or break a dish—consider how much flavor you want to add when deciding which to use.

★ **Light olive oil**—for cooking and **extra virgin olive oil** for drizzling onto salads. Flavor a bottle of good olive oil with sprigs of tarragon and garlic.
★ **Safflower or peanut oil**—for pan-frying and wok cooking.
★ **Walnut or hazelnut oil**—use in tiny amounts to add a nutty flavor to salad dressings.
★ **Sesame oil**—for seasoning Asian wok dishes, add at the end of cooking for a finishing flavor.

Seasonings and spices
These spices will add character to your cooking. Use them in small quantities and make sure they are cooked well for a smoother flavor.

★ **Fresh ginger root**—grate into, or add shavings to, Asian stir-fries and curries. Also good with ham.
★ **Red chiles**—the membranes and seeds hold most of the hotness, so remove if you don't want to add heat. The longer they are cooked, the hotter the dish will become.
★ **Lemongrass**—remove the outer leaves and simply chop the tender leaves and add to Thai stir-fries or curries.
★ **Garlic**—ideally a fresh bulb, but a jar of chopped garlic can be useful.
★ **Dried red pepper flakes**—add a powerful instant heat to a wide variety of dishes. Sprinkle onto steaks and fish.
★ **Saffron threads or powder**—add to marinades or mayonnaise. Use sparingly as a little goes a long way, or steep a pinch in hot water before adding.
★ **Sichuan peppercorns**—not from the same family as black peppercorns. Crush them and use to coat chicken or duck breasts before cooking.
★ **Whole and ground cumin and coriander**—these two spices go hand in hand and are good for giving a dish a North African flavor. Gently roast to release flavor before adding.

★ **Turmeric**—adds brilliant yellow color and an earthy flavor to Indian curries, rice, and vegetables.

★ **Ground cinnamon and cinnamon sticks**—warming spice good for savory or fruit desserts. Stir hot chocolate with a cinnamon stick.

★ **Pimentón (Spanish oak-smoked paprika)**—spice used in chorizo sausage, good for Tex-mex flavor and barbecue sauces.

★ **Cardamom**—the outer green pod is not eaten. Use in a warm fruit salad to add aromatic spice.

★ **Cayenne pepper**—this fiery spice adds flavor to dips and marinades.

★ **Garam masala**—added to Indian curries, towards the end of cooking, for extra flavor.

★ **Madras curry powder**—a sweet tangy base for an authentic South Indian curry.

★ **Chinese five-spice powder**—this Chinese wonder powder will enliven bland dishes from stir-fries to marinades.

Magic jars

These pastes, chutneys, sauces, and ketchups are a godsend for bringing variety and flair to your weekday cooking.

★ **Sweet chili sauce**—a sweet, fruity sauce. Add fresh cilantro and use as an instant dip for shrimp crackers.

★ **Hoisin sauce**—for Chinese pancakes or barbecued ribs and chicken.

★ **Plum sauce**—made from plums, apricots, and vinegar. Add to pork stir-fries or use as a marinade for chicken breasts.

★ **Good-quality mayonnaise**—good for quick dips and salad dressings.

★ **Tom yum paste**—hot and sour paste. An ideal base for making exquisite instant Thai soup.

★ **Horseradish sauce**—add to crème fraîche and spread onto roast beef sandwiches.

★ **Wasabi**—mix with soft butter and serve a dollop on grilled steak or salmon.

★ **Mango chutney**—adds zip to grilled chicken. As well as curry, it also makes a great accompaniment for cheese and crackers.

★ **Jalapeño peppers**—very hot, lovely chopped and added to a tub of store-bought guacamole. Avoid touching your face when handling them!

★ **Olive and artichoke tapenades**—spread on hot toast, bruschetta, or oat cakes for a snack.

★ **Tabasco sauce**—add a dash to a can of chopped tomatoes with scallions and cilantro for an instant tomato salsa. Adds zest to numerous dishes.

★ **Worcestershire sauce**—add to gravies, sausages, and cheese-on-toast.

★ **Tomato ketchup**—a good addition to barbecue sauces, bacon sandwiches, and Bolognese sauce.

★ **Thai curry paste**—use red or green for a speedy Thai curry or soup.

Sweet things

Your sweet cravings can be satisfied at a moment's notice with some of my favorite handy pantry standbys.

★ **75% cocoa solids dark chocolate and good-quality white chocolate**—buy the best for chocolate sauce and snacking.

★ **Good-quality cocoa powder**—tastes bitter, but gives a deep chocolate flavor to desserts and brownies. Use for dusting over desserts.

★ **Chocolate and hazelnut spread**—(such as Nutella) for making desserts and sticky toppings.

★ **Orange flower water**—for sprinkling onto fruit salads.

★ **Stem ginger in syrup**—add to whipped cream, ice cream, chocolate, and cookies.

★ **Good-quality lemon curd**—mix with cream and use as a topping for shortbread or scones.

★ **Organic dried prunes, pears, and apricots**—for tea-soaked fruits served with ice cream.

★ **Dried cranberries and cherries**—for sprinkling onto fruit tarts or stirring into plain yogurt.

★ **Biscotti or cantucci**—crisp Italian biscuits, available from Italian gourmet stores, for dunking into dessert wine or serving with coffee.

★ **Ladyfingers**—an essential ingredient for tiramisu or trifle.

★ **Amaretti or ratafia biscuits**—soaked in sherry, they can be used as a base for trifle.

★ **Sugar**—muscovado for a caramel taste; superfine, granulated, and confectioners' sugar for baking.

★ **Vanilla**—buy pure not artificial vanilla extract for a superior flavor.

★ **Marsala or Manzanilla sherry**—for poaching fruits such as figs.

In the fridge

With a few dairy ingredients to enrich and a couple of pantry staples, you have a meal in minutes.

★ **Eggs**—the ultimate convenience food. Always have some on hand for scrambled eggs, omelets, and frittatas.

★ **Milk**—choose organic low-fat.

★ **Unsalted butter**—has a much more refined flavor and is better for cooking.

★ **Plain Greek yogurt or bio yogurt**—yogurt is very good for adding to curries, or making into dips or quick desserts.

★ **Block of Parmesan cheese**—for grating as you need it on pasta, pizza, or salads.

★ **Crème fraiche or heavy cream**—use to enrich sauces or as an accompaniment for sweet things.

★ **Mascarpone cheese**—this rich cream cheese can make an instant ice cream or tiramisù.

In the freezer

Keep your freezer stocked with foods that can be quickly cooked from frozen—an enormous asset to the time-poor cook.

★ **Fresh chicken and fish stocks**—for gravies, risotto, and cooking rice. Avoid bouillon cubes—instead freeze fresh stock in ice-cube trays.

★ **Good-quality ice cream and sorbet**—store a good-quality vanilla ice cream and a lemon sorbet for an instant dessert.

★ **Mixed summer berries**—great for quick desserts in the winter months.

★ **Mixed seafood and shrimp**—can be added to stir-fry dishes without defrosting.

★ **Pastry**—puff and filo are essential for a variety of quick savory and sweet dishes.

★ **Fish fillets**—keep a variety of frozen fish, such as tuna, cod, and haddock.

★ **Frozen vegetables**—if you haven't had a chance to shop for vegetables, make sure you have some in your freezer, such as green beans, baby peas, corn kernels, and spinach.

★ **Frozen chicken breasts**—cut into strips before freezing for quick defrosting.

★ **Ready-to-bake focaccia and ciabatta bread**—a handy standby to accompany meals or for making garlic bread.

no-cook deli dinners

almost-instant dishes

deli pasta

As far as a healthy quick meal goes, you can't beat a bowl of home-cooked pasta. Keep your refrigerator well stocked with a few key deli ingredients and a sustaining, comforting dinner is never far from your table. My advice is to buy good-quality dried pasta in a variety of shapes and sizes. The only fresh pastas worth buying for everyday eating are filled varieties, such as ravioli or tortelloni. Always keep a piece of fresh Parmesan cheese in the refrigerator for grating over your chosen pasta dish.

pappardelle with artichoke hearts and prosciutto

This is a quick and simple midweek dinner that uses a tub of crème fraîche and some great storebought ingredients to create a luxurious pasta dish that even non-cooks can make. If you can't find pappardelle, it will work just as well with tagliatelle.

8 oz. dried pappardelle (thick ribbons of pasta)

1 cup crème fraîche or heavy cream

1 garlic clove, crushed

1 teaspoon Dijon mustard

5 oz. roasted and marinated artichoke hearts, drained and cut into small pieces

6 slices (about 1½ oz.) prosciutto, cut into strips

sea salt and freshly ground black pepper

¼ cup finely freshly grated Parmesan cheese, to serve

Serves 2

Bring a large pan of salted water to a boil. Add the pasta, cover, and bring back to a boil. Remove the lid, stir the pasta, and cook according to the packet instructions. The pasta is ready when it is tender but with a central resistance to the bite—*al dente*. When cooked, tip into a colander and drain well, reserving a little of the cooking water.

Add the crème fraîche, garlic, and mustard to the pan and bring to a boil. Add the cooked pasta, artichokes, and prosciutto and stir everything together, thinning with a little of the reserved pasta cooking water if necessary. Season to taste with pepper.

Spoon the pasta into warmed serving bowls and sprinkle with Parmesan cheese. Serve immediately.

More quick deli pasta ideas:

★ Spicy tomato fusilli—half-dried tomatoes, crushed garlic, thinly chopped red chile, shredded fresh basil, and chile oil or extra virgin olive oil, tossed through cooked fusilli pasta.

★ Creamy salmon and pea linguine—hot-smoked salmon flakes, salmon roe, cooked petit pois, thinly chopped fresh dill, and crème fraîche, stirred into linguine pasta.

★ Sweet pepper and anchovy penne—roasted bell peppers, chopped marinated anchovies, red pepper flakes, and chopped fresh parsley, added to cooked penne pasta.

★ Creamy bacon and mushroom spaghetti—cubes of cooked bacon, chopped marinated wild mushrooms, crushed garlic, and crème fraîche, with cooked spaghetti.

★ Cheese and spinach penne—crumbled firm goat cheese, chopped pitted black olives, baby spinach leaves, and a drizzle of extra virgin olive oil, tossed through cooked penne pasta.

★ deli pizza

Freshly made pizza is delicious and surprisingly simple to assemble once you know how to make the most of all the fantastic foods you can buy at your local deli counter.

Keep some ready-made frozen or long-life pizza crusts and a few tubs of any basic tomato pasta sauce in your pantry. To assemble a super-speedy pizza, first preheat your oven to 400°F and put a baking sheet in to heat. Next, take a pizza crust and spread it generously with the pasta sauce. Select your deli ingredients (see opposite page) and chop or slice them as necessary. Arrange these on the prepared pizza base and season with a little salt and pepper. When your pizza is assembled, carefully slide it onto the baking sheet and place it in the preheated oven. Cook for 10–12 minutes, or until the crust is starting to brown at the edges and all the ingredients are warmed through. Drizzle with extra virgin olive oil or a flavored oil such as hot pepper, garlic, or truffle and grate or shave some fresh Parmesan cheese over the top. Serve with a small bowl of dressed salad leaves—arugula or baby leaf salad are both ideal.

Quick deli pizza ideas—use an 8 to 10-inch pizza base per person. Spread the base with your chosen sauce topping and choose a selection of flavors from below:

★ Garlicky mushroom pizza—marinated mushrooms, slices of Talleggio cheese, and slivers of smoked garlic.

★ Marinara pizza—antipasti-style marinated seafood (usually a mixture of cooked squid, mussels, and shrimp), capers, and slices of garlic butter. Add a generous handful of fresh arugula to the pizza once it's cooked.

★ Mediterraneo pizza—sliced balsamic onions, cubes of feta cheese, pitted black olives, marinated anchovy fillets, and a sprinkle of dried mixed herbs or *herbes de Provence*.

★ Italian salami pizza—slices of Neopolitan salami or any other Italian-style salami, pitted black olives, half-dried tomatoes, thinly sliced red onion, and a few spoonfuls of pesto.

★ Tuna and artichoke pizza—a small can of tuna in olive oil, marinated artichoke hearts, roasted bell peppers, thinly sliced red onion, and slices of buffalo mozzarella cheese.

★ Vegetarian pizza—slices of grilled eggplant or courgette, roasted bell peppers, ricotta cheese, toasted pine nuts, and shredded fresh basil leaves.

★ Spinach and prosciutto pizza—spread baby spinach leaves over a tomato base, then cover with thin slices of prosciutto and thick slices of mozzarella cheese.

★ Creamy bacon pizza—cooked bacon cubes, a few spoonfuls of mascarpone cheese, thinly sliced red onion, and a sprinkle of dried thyme and grated Parmesan cheese.

★ Chicken and blue cheese pizza—shredded roasted chicken breast sprinkled over a base spread with pesto, thinly sliced red onions, cubed Gorgonzola, Dolcelatte, or other blue cheese, and chopped walnuts.

deli platters

Sharing a deli platter is an effortless and sociable way of eating for busy people. Ask to sample a new cheese or salami before buying at the deli counter and eat French-style by following with a bowl of salad leaves to cleanse the palate. Arrange the foods you choose on large serving platters and make sure there is plenty of interesting bread on offer. Choose specialty breads such as Irish soda, baguette, ciabatta, focaccia, bagels, rye, walnut, or olive bread, or *grissini* (bread sticks).

mixed meats platter

On French and Italian menus you will often find a *charcuterie* or *affettato* platter displaying an array of dried and cured meats. The celeriac remoulade can be made ahead of time and refrigerated.

3½ oz. Neopolitan salami or chorizo sausage
4 slices of prosciutto or Serrano ham
2 oz. marinated olives (black, green, or mixed)
2 oz. mini gherkins or caperberries, drained and rinsed
2 big handfuls arugula

For the celeriac remoulade
1 celeriac (about 8 oz.), peeled
freshly squeezed juice of ½ lemon
2 tablespoons good-quality mayonnaise
1 teaspoon Dijon mustard
2 tablespoons chopped fresh tarragon
sea salt and freshly ground black pepper

Serves 2

First make the remoulade. Cut the celeriac into matchstick-sized pieces or, if you find it easier, roughly grate it. Place in a bowl of cold water with the lemon juice to prevent discoloration.

Bring a pan of cold water to a boil, then plunge in the drained celeriac and cook for 1 minute, drain and refresh with cold water, then drain again. Lightly pat dry with a clean kitchen towel or some paper towels. Put the mayonnaise, mustard, and tarragon in a large bowl and mix thoroughly. Season to taste with salt and pepper. Toss the dried celeriac in the dressing until well coated.

Arrange the cured meats on a large serving platter with the olives, and gherkins or caperberries and heap the celeriac remoulade in the center. Serve the arugula in a separate bowl.

More quick deli platter ideas:

★ Italian-style *antipasti* platter—arrange roasted bell peppers, roasted and marinated artichoke hearts, tomatoes, and mini mozzarella balls or slices of buffalo mozzarella cheese on a large platter and sprinkle with torn fresh basil. Add caperberries and marinated anchovy fillets. Serve with grilled ciabatta slices rubbed with garlic or some focaccia and a mixed baby leaf salad.

★ Swedish-style smoked fish platter—choose a variety of smoked fish such as hot-smoked salmon, smoked eel, smoked trout, smoked haddock, and salmon gravlax. Accompany with a salad made by tossing peeled and thinly sliced cucumber and shredded fennel with chopped fresh dill and a drop of white wine vinegar. Serve with toasted rye bread or warmed blinis spread with sour cream.

★ Mixed seafood platter—choose a selection of fresh seafood from the fish counter at your supermarket such as marinated seafood (usually a mixture of cooked squid, mussels, and shrimp), dressed crab, shell-on tiger shrimp, cooked and halved lobster, opened oysters, and green-lipped mussels. Arrange your selection on a platter with some crushed ice. Garnish with fresh lemon and lime wedges. Serve with a bowl of aioli (pages 97 and 143) and slices of warmed baguette. Don't forget to provide plenty of serviettes.

★ Cheese platter—there are so many fabulous cheeses available; choose a selection of your favorites. A good combination is a ripe Brie de Meaux, a tangy Spanish Manchego, a blue Dolcelatte or Gorgonzola, and a fresh goat cheese. Serve with slices of ripe pear, black grapes, or sticks of celery. Add sweet balsamic onions, a good-quality red onion chutney, or quince jelly (membrillo), and serve with slices of walnut bread.

This light salad is simplicity itself to prepare. All you need to do is use the best-quality ingredients you can find. Look out at the deli counter for roasted red and yellow bell peppers and eggplant, but if you can't find them, use ones that are preserved in oil and sold in jars. Do drain them well before using as they can be rather oily.

It makes sense to toast a large batch of pine nuts and keep them in an airtight container so they are ready to add when needed to salads or pizza or pasta dishes.

roasted bell pepper and eggplant salad

1 tablespoon pine nuts

5 oz. mixed greens

3½ oz. roasted bell peppers, sliced

3½ oz. roasted eggplant, sliced

2 oz. feta or firm goat cheese, crumbled

a handful of fresh basil leaves, shredded

2 tablespoons extra virgin olive oil

freshly ground black pepper

Italian bread, to serve

Serves 2

First toast the pine nuts. Spread out a tablespoonful (or more if toasting a batch) in a thin layer on the base of a large, nonstick frying pan and place over a low heat. Cook over low to medium heat for 2–3 minutes, gently tossing them frequently until they are golden brown. Remove from the heat and set aside until needed.

Put the greens, bell peppers, eggplant, toasted pine nuts, cheese, and basil in a large bowl. Add the olive oil, season well with pepper, and toss until evenly coated with the seasoned oil.

Arrange the prepared salad on serving plates and serve immediately with a basket of good Italian bread, such as ciabatta or Pugliese.

Variation: Add a few slices of prosciutto and some pitted black olives to the salad.

If you've had a busy day and are home too late for a heavy meal, then this snack dinner is ideal. Enjoy it with a glass of chilled chardonnay or other white white.

Gravlax is a Swedish speciality—very fresh, raw salmon fillet is cured with dill, sugar, salt, and coarse peppercorns. It is often available in supermarkets and sometimes packed with a sachet of dill-flavored mustard sauce, which can be rather overpowering. I like to mix a tablespoon of the sauce with two tablespoons of crème fraîche or sour cream.

gravlax and pickled cucumber open sandwich

1 cucumber

1 teaspoon white wine vinegar

½ teaspoon chopped fresh dill

freshly ground black pepper (or mixed peppercorns)

2 slices of rye bread

2 tablespoons crème fraîche or sour cream

3½ oz. gravlax

Serves 2

Peel the cucumber and halve it lengthwise. Scoop out the seeds using a teaspoon and cut it into wafer-thin, crescent-shaped slices. Pat these dry with paper towels and put them in a large bowl.

Put the vinegar and chopped dill in a small bowl, season with a little pepper (or mixed peppercorns), and use a fork to combine. Pour the dressing over the cucumber and toss to coat.

Lightly toast the bread and, while it's still warm, spread generously with crème fraîche or sour cream. Top with the marinated cucumber salad and slices of gravlax. Serve immediately with the remaining crème fraîche separately.

Strictly speaking, this isn't a "no-cook" recipe since the potatoes need to be boiled. But if you are really short of time, buy a tub of good-quality ready-made potato salad and mix it with half the amount of the dill dressing.

For a variation, I sometimes use Swedish pickled herrings instead of smoked trout—they give the dish even more Swedish style.

After opening a bottle of beer for the dressing, it would seem wasteful not to enjoy a glass of it with the salad!

smoked trout, warm new potato, and beet salad

4 oz. small new potatoes, scrubbed and halved if large

sea salt and freshly ground black pepper

For the dill dressing

1 teaspoon grainy mustard

1 tablespoon beer

1 teaspoon sugar

2 tablespoons extra virgin olive oil

2 tablespoons chopped fresh dill, plus extra sprigs to garnish

4 oz. smoked trout fillets, skinned and flaked

2 cooked fresh beets (not pickled), sliced into wedges

1 head of endive, thickly sliced

whole-wheat bread or similar, to serve

Put the potatoes in a large pan, add sufficient cold water to cover, add a little salt, and bring to a boil. Cook for 10–15 minutes until just tender.

Meanwhile, make the dressing. Put the mustard, beer or lager, sugar, olive oil, and chopped dill in a small bowl and use a small whisk or fork to combine.

Drain the potatoes and, when cool enough to handle, slice thickly and put in a bowl with half of the dressing. Toss to coat.

Arrange the trout fillet flakes, slices of warm dressed potato, beet wedges, and endive on serving plates and garnish with dill sprigs. Drizzle the remaining dressing over the top and serve immediately with slices of warm whole-wheat bread or similar.

Serves 2

This makes a lovely change from shrimp cocktail. Buy the juiciest-looking cooked shrimp you can find and leave them in the marinade for as long as possible. I use pink grapefruit as it looks prettier and tastes sweeter than the white variety.

spicy tiger shrimp salad

1 garlic clove, crushed

freshly squeezed juice of 1 lime

2 tablespoons sweet chili sauce

7 oz. cooked tiger shrimp, peeled but tails left intact

1 pink grapefruit

2 tablespoons extra virgin olive oil

¾ cup cherry tomatoes, halved

1 small ripe avocado, peeled, pitted, and diced

½ red onion, thinly sliced

a handful of fresh cilantro leaves

garlic bread or similar, to serve

Serves 2

Put the garlic, lime juice, and sweet chili sauce in a shallow container and whisk with a fork to combine. Add the shrimp, stir to coat with the mixture, cover, and set aside to marinate while you prepare the rest of the salad.

Cut away the peel and pith from the grapefruit with a serrated knife. Hold the grapefruit in the palm of your hand and cut away each segment, working over a large bowl to catch the juices.

Add the olive oil to the grapefruit juice and whisk with a fork to combine. Add the grapefruit segments, cherry tomatoes, avocado, red onion, and cilantro to the bowl and toss to combine.

Divide the prepared salad between serving plates, or glasses for a cocktail effect. Remove the shrimp from their marinade (using tongs or a slotted spoon) and arrange them on top. Drizzle the remaining marinade over the salad. Serve immediately with slices of warm garlic bread or similar.

This combination of smoked chicken, mango, fresh cilantro, and lime makes an irresistible summer salad. Since there is no need to cook the chicken, all that's left to do is to make the dressing and assemble the other ingredients.

This recipe would also work well if you have a few friends coming over—use a whole smoked chicken (about 3 lb. in weight) and double the remaining ingredients. If you can't find smoked chicken, use a mixture of cooked chicken and smoked ham instead.

smoked chicken, mango, and lime salad

1 large ripe mango

juice and finely grated zest of 1 lime

3 tablespoons light olive oil

1 tablespoon finely chopped fresh cilantro, plus extra sprigs to garnish

2 boneless smoked chicken breasts (about 12 oz. total weight)

romaine lettuce leaves

1 scallion, thinly sliced

sea salt and freshly ground black pepper

extra virgin olive oil, to serve

Serves 2

Remove the skin and stone of the mango, then chop the flesh. Put in a food processor or blender with the lime juice, blitz until smooth, then gradually add the olive oil in a thin stream with the motor running until the mixture begins to thicken. Pour the dressing into a large bowl and stir in the chopped cilantro and lime zest.

Slice the chicken into bite-sized pieces and put it in the bowl with the dressing. Toss the chicken until coated in the dressing. Arrange the lettuce leaves on serving plates, drizzle with a little extra virgin olive oil, and season with salt and pepper.

Spoon the chicken with the mango dressing over the leaves and scatter with the scallion slices and cilantro sprigs to finish. Serve immediately.

Picking up a hot rotisserie-cooked chicken from a supermarket is the perfect answer for commuters and busy parents. The warm chicken flesh slightly softens the cheese, making the salad taste even more delectable, so do try and get your chicken home quickly and use it while it's still warm!

This is good salad to serve at Christmas, when you can use Stilton cheese and leftover turkey instead of chicken.

roast chicken, watercress, and blue cheese salad

1 small roasted chicken (weighing about 2¾ lb.)

3 oz. watercress

1 heart of romaine lettuce, chopped

½ cup walnut pieces

1 red dessert apple, quartered, cored, and thinly sliced

sea salt and freshly ground black pepper

freshly squeezed juice of ½ lemon

1 tablespoon extra virgin olive oil

2 oz. firm blue cheese such as Gorgonzola, cut into cubes

1 baguette, to serve

Serves 2

Remove the meat from the roast chicken carcass, including the wings and the legs. Cut it into bite-sized pieces.

Put the chicken pieces in a bowl with the watercress sprigs, lettuce, walnut pieces, and apple slices. Season well and add the lemon juice and olive oil. Toss well so that the salad is evenly coated with the dressing.

Divide the dressed salad between serving plates and arrange the cheese cubes among the leaves. Serve immediately with generous slices of warm baguette.

simple dishes
fuss-free recipes for two

Couscous is an excellent pantry staple for the busy cook since it doesn't need cooking—it is simply soaked in water or stock and fluffed up with a fork. Couscous is classically served with a rich North African stew prepared in a tagine as it acts like an absorbent sponge and mops up the sauce. This roasted vegetable couscous is spicy and satisfying.

moroccan-style roasted vegetable couscous

2 small red onions

1 sweet potato

2 small bell peppers

2 small leeks

2 garlic cloves, halved

2 tablespoons olive oil

½ teaspoon dried red pepper flakes

1¼ cups couscous

1¼ cups hot vegetable stock or water

a handful of fresh mint sprigs

freshly squeezed lemon juice, to taste

sea salt and freshly ground black pepper

a non-stick baking sheet or small roasting tin

Serves 2

Preheat the oven to 400°F.

Remove the skin from the onions and slice them into thin wedges. Peel the sweet potato and cut into chunks. Core and seed the bell peppers, then chop. Trim the leeks, then split them and wash them well. Dry with paper towels, and cut into large chunks.

Put the prepared vegetables and garlic on a nonstick baking sheet or in in a small roasting pan. Pour the olive oil over the top, add the pepper flakes and use your hands to toss the vegetables until they are coated with the oil mixture. Place the pan in the preheated oven and cook for about 20–25 minutes, or until golden and tender.

Meanwhile, put the couscous in a large bowl and pour over the hot vegetable stock or water. Cover and set aside until the couscous swells and absorbs all the liquid, about 10 minutes.

Use a fork to fluff up the couscous, then add the roasted vegetables and mint sprigs. Add a little lemon juice and season to taste. Serve immediately whilst still warm.

Variation: Add 2 oz. crumbled or diced feta cheese to the couscous.

You can keep things simple when preparing this dish by cooking the broccoli in the same pan as the pasta. If it's in season, use purple sprouting broccoli; trim the fibrous ends, then slice into ½-inch lengths, dividing the florets into bite-sized pieces. The anchovy is already very salty, so it's best to taste a forkful before adding any more salt.

tagliatelle with broccoli, anchovy, parmesan, and crème fraîche

4 oz. dried tagliatelle

10 oz. broccoli florets

1 tablespoon olive oil

2 garlic cloves, crushed

½ teaspoon dried red pepper flakes

3 anchovy fillets, roughly chopped

½ cup crème fraîche or heavy cream

sea salt and freshly ground black pepper

freshly grated Parmesan cheese, to serve

Serves 2

Bring a large pan of salted water to a boil. Add the pasta, cover, and bring to a boil. Remove the lid, stir the pasta, and cook according to the package instructions. Add the broccoli to the pasta 3–4 minutes before the end of cooking. Drain the pasta and the broccoli well and reserve a little of the cooking water.

Wipe out the pan and add the olive oil. Cook the garlic, pepper flakes, and anchovies over low heat for about 2 minutes. Add the crème fraîche, season with a little pepper, and bring to a boil. Return the cooked broccoli and pasta to the pan, adding a little of the reserved cooking water if necessary to thin the sauce down. Season to taste with pepper.

Divide the pasta between serving bowls and serve immediately, sprinkled with Parmesan cheese.

Halloumi is a firm Greek cheese that is delicious eaten when hot and melting. It has a reasonably long shelf-life before it is opened, which means you can keep a pack tucked away in the refrigerator. Harissa is a fiery chile paste used in North African cooking—add more if you like your food spicy.

1 tablespoon olive oil

1 onion, thinly chopped

1 garlic clove, crushed

1 tablespoon harissa paste
(see note below)

14-oz. can chickpeas, drained

14-oz. can chopped tomatoes
(flavored with garlic or mixed herbs,
if available)

4 oz. halloumi cheese, cut into cubes

3½ oz. baby spinach leaves

sea salt and freshly ground
black pepper

freshly squeezed juice of ½ lemon

freshly grated Parmesan cheese and
crisp green side salad, to serve

Serves 2

harissa-spiced chickpeas
with halloumi and spinach

Pour the oil into a large pan and gently sauté the onion and garlic until softened. Add the harissa paste, chickpeas, and chopped tomatoes. Bring to a boil and let simmer for about 5 minutes.

Add the halloumi cheese and spinach, cover, and cook over a low heat for a further 5 minutes. Season to taste and stir in the lemon juice. Spoon onto serving plates and sprinkle with the Parmesan cheese. Serve immediately with a crisp green side salad.

Variation: Substitute mixed beans (such as borlotti, kidney, and cannellini) for the chickpeas.

Note: If you don't have harissa paste, you can make your own by mixing together ½ teaspoon cayenne pepper, 1 tablespoon ground cumin, 1 tablespoon tomato paste, and the freshly squeezed juice of 1 lime.

Risotto is a relatively simple dish to make. You have to watch the rice like a hawk and a good deal of stirring is required, but you can multi-task and rustle up a salad while it's cooking! Remember to keep the stock nice and hot and the heat constant. Roasting the squash first brings out its sweetness and the pumpkin seeds add a spicy crunch.

roasted butternut squash risotto

1 lb. butternut squash, peeled, seeded, and diced

3 tablespoons olive oil

1½ teaspoons dried red pepper flakes

sea salt and freshly ground black pepper

2 tablespoons pumpkin seeds

3½ cups vegetable stock

1 small onion, thinly chopped

¾ cup Arborio rice

½ cup white wine

½ cup Parmesan cheese, finely grated

crème fraîche or sour cream, to serve

Serves 2

Preheat the oven to 450°F.

Put the butternut squash in a small roasting pan with 1 tablespoon of the olive oil and ½ teaspoon of the pepper flakes and season well. Toss the squash in the seasoned oil until it is evenly coated. Put in the preheated oven and cook for about 20 minutes, or until soft and golden. (Use a large spoon to turn the squash at regular intervals while it is cooking.)

Heat 1 tablespoon of the remaining olive oil in a small skillet and toast the pumpkin seeds with the remaining pepper flakes for about 1–2 minutes until lightly browned. Set aside until needed.

While the squash is cooking in the oven, make the risotto. Pour the vegetable stock into a large pan and heat to a simmer. Pour the remaining oil into a high-sided pan and gently sauté the onion over medium heat for about 1 minute, or until softened. Add the rice, stir for 2–3 minutes, then add the wine and let simmer until reduced by half. Add another ladleful of hot stock. Let the risotto continue to simmer gently, adding another ladleful or two of stock each time the liquid has been absorbed into the rice. Stir, almost continuously, until the rice has absorbed all the stock.

Once the rice is cooked and tender, stir in the roasted butternut squash and the Parmesan cheese and season to taste with salt and pepper. Serve immediately, topped with a little crème fraîche or sour cream and sprinkled with the toasted pumpkin seeds.

A bag of mixed seafood in the freezer is a great standby for a fast dinner. It can be added frozen to rice dishes, pasta, or soup—just make sure the dishes are cooked for an extra few minutes and are piping hot before serving.

stir-fried seafood with vegetables and a balsamic dressing

2 tablespoons olive oil

1 bell pepper, cored, seeded, and cut into thin strips

2 leeks, trimmed and cut into strips

1 large onion, cut into thick wedges

5 oz. cherry tomatoes, halved

2 garlic cloves, thinly sliced

1 teaspoon dried red pepper flakes

10 oz. frozen mixed seafood, such as shrimp, mussels, scallops, and squid rings, either defrosted or frozen

2 teaspoons balsamic vinegar

a few fresh cilantro sprigs, to garnish

a large skillet or wok

Serves 2

Heat 1 tablespoon of the oil in a large skillet or wok. Add the bell pepper, leeks, and onion and stir-fry over high heat until lightly brown. Add the cherry tomatoes and cook for a further 2 minutes. Remove the vegetables from the pan and set aside in a warm place until needed.

Heat the remaining oil in the same skillet or wok. Add the pepper flakes, garlic, and mixed seafood and stir-fry over high heat. Cook for 3–4 minutes, stirring occasionally (increase the cooking time to 7–8 minutes if the seafood is frozen).

Mix the warm vegetables with the seafood and add the balsamic vinegar and cilantro at the last moment. Serve immediately.

If you have ever tasted the classic French fish soup *bouillabaisse* and enjoyed the flavor, then this is a good cheat's version. The combination of saffron, orange, and fennel gives the stew its distinctive flavor. If you don't have dry vermouth on hand, use dry Martini or a dry white wine in its place. If you have time to make the base of the stew the day before you plan to eat it, the flavors will develop even further—simply cook the fish at the last moment.

mediterranean chunky fish
stew with cheese toasts

In a large pan, gently sauté the onion, crushed garlic, thyme, and fennel in the olive oil for about 6–8 minutes, or until soft. Add the dry vermouth, dry Martini, or dry white wine and let bubble, uncovered, until the liquid has reduced to almost nothing.

Add the tomato paste, saffron, orange juice and pared rind, and 1 cup cold water. Raise the heat and cook for 10 minutes. Add the cod fillet and cook gently for a further 2 minutes, then taste, and season if necessary.

Meanwhile, preheat the broiler to high. Rub the baguette slices with garlic and toast on each side under the broiler until lightly golden. Sprinkle with the grated cheese (optional).

Ladle the stew into warmed deep serving bowls and balance the cheese-topped toasts on top. Serve immediately.

1 small onion, thinly chopped

2 garlic cloves, 1 crushed; 1 left whole and unpeeled, halved

a pinch of dried thyme

1 small bulb fennel, hard core removed and thinly chopped

1 tablespoon olive oil

3 tablespoons dry vermouth, preferably Noilly Prat, or dry white wine

2 cups tomato paste

1 pinch of saffron threads

freshly squeezed juice of 1 orange, plus a strip of pared rind

7 oz. skinless cod fillet, cut into large chunks

sea salt and freshly ground black pepper

4 thin slices of baguette

2 oz. Emmental or Gruyère cheese, grated

Serves 2

Rather than brown the chicken breast in a pan, you simply season it and let the oven do all the work. There is a lot of garlic in this dish, but the flavor becomes much more subtle once the garlic is blanched.

roast chicken with garlic, apple, and cider

4 garlic cloves, peeled but left whole

2 chicken breasts with skin (each weighing about 6 oz.), pounded if thick

sea salt and freshly ground black pepper

2 tablespoons olive oil

½ cup hard apple cider

1 Golden Delicious apple, peeled, quartered, and diced

2 tablespoons Dijon mustard

½ cup crème fraîche or heavy cream

a handful of chopped fresh parsley

broccoli spears and new potatoes, to serve

a baking sheet

Serves 2

Preheat the oven to 400°F.

Bring a small pan of water to a boil and cook the garlic cloves for 2–3 minutes, or until tender. Drain and set aside until needed.

Season the chicken breasts and drizzle with the olive oil. Put them on a baking sheet and place on the top shelf of the preheated oven to cook for about 25 minutes, or until the chicken is cooked through and the skin is golden.

Meanwhile, put the garlic, cider, chopped apple, and mustard in a large skillet. Cook gently over a low heat for about 10 minutes.

When the chicken is cooked, remove it from the oven and transfer to the pan. Add the crème fraîche or heavy cream to the pan and simmer for 5 minutes. Use the back of a fork to squash the garlic down into the sauce, taking care not to squash the apples too. Season to taste. Stir in the parsley and serve immediately, with broccoli spears and new potatoes.

Variations: This classic French sauce also works well with oven-roasted or grilled pork chops. Pour a little of the sauce over cooked tagliatelle and toss until the pasta is evenly coated; serve this instead of new potatoes with the chicken or pork.

You can add your choice of vegetables to this basic curry recipe, such as sliced mushrooms, trimmed green beans, fresh spinach, bamboo shoots, or sticks of zucchini and carrots—it's perfect for using up odds and ends from the fridge. Jasmine or fragrant rice is a delicately scented white rice native to Thailand. If you are very short on time, use one of the excellent brands that can be microwaved in the packet.

quick thai chicken curry

1¾ cup coconut milk

3 tablespoons Thai green curry paste

1 tablespoon safflower oil

1 chicken breast (weighing about 14 oz.), cut into bite-sized pieces

1 teaspoon grated lime zest

1 teaspoon Thai fish sauce

4 oz. mixed fresh vegetables of your choice (see above)

a handful of fresh basil leaves

For the jasmine rice

1 cup Thai jasmine or fragrant rice

2 tablespoons unsalted butter

a pinch of sea salt

a large skillet or wok

Serves 2

To make the jasmine rice, put the rice in a large pan that has a tight-fitting lid. Add 1½ cups cold water and the butter and salt. Bring to a boil, then turn down the heat to a simmer. Cook over low heat, covered, for 20 minutes, or until the rice has absorbed all the liquid (add a little more water if the rice is not yet tender).

Meanwhile, pour the coconut milk into a saucepan and gently bring it to near boiling. Remove the saucepan from the heat and stir in the Thai curry paste. Put to one side.

Pour the oil into a large skillet or wok and stir-fry the chicken pieces over high heat until golden, about 2 minutes.

Pour the warm, spiced coconut milk over the fried chicken pieces and add the lime zest and fish sauce. Add any vegetables you are using at this stage. Stir and simmer gently for about 12 minutes, or until everything is cooked through.

Remove the cooked rice from the heat and let sit for 5 minutes. Fluff it up with a fork just before serving.

Scatter the basil over the curry and serve it with a small bowl of the rice on the side.

The juiciness of the grilled tomatoes gives the meat a natural sauce and the creamy soft polenta makes a great alternative to mashed potatoes. Using a fresh chicken stock will make all the difference to the flavor of the polenta.

The trick to a tender steak is to take the meat out of the fridge 15 minutes before you intend to cook it, then make sure you cook the meat fast over a scorchingly high heat.

beef steak with goat cheese polenta and grilled tomatoes

1¼ cups chicken stock

2½ oz. instant polenta

2 tablespoons unsalted butter

2½ oz. firm goat cheese, crumbled

sea salt and freshly ground black pepper

a crisp green salad, to serve

4 plum tomatoes

1 tablespoon extra virgin olive oil

a few drops of balsamic vinegar

2 sirloin, rump, or fillet steaks (each weighing about 6 oz.)

a crisp, green salad, to serve

a heavy-based skillet or griddle pan

Serves 2

Pour the chicken stock into a large pan and bring it to a boil. Remove from the heat and slowly add the polenta, pouring from a pitcher and whisking until all of it has been added. Return the pan to the heat and cook until the polenta thickens and falls away from the side of the pan. Beat in the butter and goat cheese and season to taste with salt and pepper.

Cut the tomatoes in half lengthwise and sprinkle with salt and pepper. Heat the oil in a heavy-based skillet or griddle pan and cook for 2 minutes on one side before turning them over and cooking briefly on the other side. Drizzle with the balsamic vinegar. Remove from the pan and set aside in a warm place.

Season the steaks on both sides. Place a heavy-based broiler pan over high heat until very hot indeed. Quickly drop each steak directly in the pan. Sear quickly on both sides. Turn the heat down and cook them for 2–3 minutes on each side (for medium rare—see guide on page 58).

Lift the steaks onto warmed serving plates and add a few generous spoonfuls of the polenta and the grilled tomatoes. Serve with a green salad.

This is a cheat's version of a Spanish peasant stew called a *fabada*—beans, sausage, and a rich tomato and red wine sauce make a welcoming dinner on a cold winter's evening. If you can't get hold of chorizo, any spicy sausage will do. It is especially good with a glass of Spanish Rioja.

spanish sausage and butter bean tagine

1 tablespoon olive oil

1 onion, thinly chopped

2 garlic cloves, crushed

2½ oz. chorizo sausage, skin removed and cut into ½-inch slices

½ cup red wine

14-oz. can of chopped tomatoes

1 red onion, cut into thin petals

14-oz. can butter beans, drained

1 teaspoon dried mixed herbs

a few fresh rosemary or thyme sprigs

sea salt and freshly ground black pepper

2 tablespoons of finely, freshly grated Parmesan cheese

warm crusty bread, to serve

a large high-sided skillet

Serves 2

Heat the oil in a large, high-sided skillet. Add the onions and garlic and cook for a few minutes over medium heat. Add the chorizo and cook for a further 2–3 minutes.

Add the red wine and bring to a boil. Let bubble until the mixture is reduced by half. Add the chopped tomatoes, red onion petals, butter beans, ½ cup water, and the dried mixed herbs and rosemary or thyme sprigs. Simmer, uncovered, for about 10 minutes.

Season to taste with salt and pepper and spoon into warmed serving bowls. Sprinkle with the Parmesan cheese and serve immediately with chunks of warm crusty bread to mop up the juices.

A frittata, Italy's version of an open omelet, is one of the most convenient ways to use up leftovers. This one is packed with roasted peppers and pepperoni and must be served immediately—otherwise it goes on cooking and loses its soft creaminess. The frittata can also be left to cool, cut into wedges, and enjoyed as part of a lunch-on-the-go the following day.

pepperoni, bell pepper, and croûton frittata

4 eggs

sea salt and freshly ground black pepper

1 oz. grated Gruyère cheese

1 scallion, thinly sliced

2 tablespoons unsalted butter

2 oz. firm white bread, torn into small pieces

1 garlic clove, crushed

1 oz. pepperoni, sliced

1 roasted bell pepper, cut into strips

a crisp green or tomato and basil salad, to serve

a medium-sized ovenproof skillet

Serves 2

Break the eggs into a bowl and beat well using a fork. Season well with salt and pepper and add the scallion and half the cheese. Mix well.

Melt half the butter in a medium-sized, ovenproof skillet. Add the pieces of bread and toss them for 2–3 minutes over heat until golden brown and crispy. Remove from the heat and set aside.

Preheat the broiler. Add the remaining butter and the garlic to the pan, and when the butter starts to froth, add the beaten eggs. Turn the heat down and leave the eggs to cook gently for a few minutes. Arrange the pepperoni and pepper strips on the top and sprinkle with the remaining grated cheese and reserved croutons.

Put the skillet under the preheated broiler and cook for a further 2–3 minutes until the frittatta is puffed and just set but still wobbly. Remove from the broiler and serve immediately with a green or tomato and basil salad.

Variation: Also delicious made with any combination of the following: crumbled firm goat cheese, sliced mushrooms, baby spinach leaves, zucchini, and sliced cooked potatoes.

These delicious little pancake rolls could not be easier to make. Chinese pancakes are available in Asian grocers and many supermarkets, but if you can't find them use small flour tortillas or ready-made "batter" pancakes.

chinese duck pancakes

2 duck breasts with skin (each weighing about 5 oz.)

2 teaspoons sea salt flakes

1 teaspoon Chinese five-spice powder

6–8 Chinese pancakes or small flour tortillas or 4 ready-made "batter" pancakes

1 scallion, thinly sliced

½ cucumber, seeded, and thinly sliced

a handful of fresh cilantro sprigs, finely chopped

1 small red chile, thinly chopped

4 tablespoons hoisin or plum sauce

an oven-proof skillet

Serves 2

Preheat the oven to 400°F.

Rub the skin of the duck breasts with the salt and Chinese five-spice powder. Heat an ovenproof skillet and cook the breasts skin-side down until golden. Place the skillet in the oven and continue to cook the breast for a further 10–15 minutes or until tender but still pink in the center.

To serve, either steam the pancakes or place in the microwave for a few minutes until piping hot (check the instructions on the package).

Slice the duck breasts and finely shred the meat. Place it on a warmed serving plate. Arrange the cucumber, scallion, cilantro sprigs, chile, and hoisin sauce in little bowls.

To serve, dig in and help yourselves. Take a warm Chinese pancake or small tortilla (or half of a "batter" pancake) and spread it with a teaspoonful of sauce. Place some duck, scallion, cucumber, cilantro, and chile in the center, roll up, and eat with your fingers.

This simple recipe is bursting with Greek flavors. If you marinate any meat in yogurt, it becomes incredibly tender, so the longer you can leave it in before cooking the better.

minted lamb pitas with red onion and tomato salad

3 tablespoons Greek yogurt

1 garlic clove, crushed

2 tablespoons finely chopped fresh mint, plus extra leaves for the salad

a squeeze of fresh lemon juice, plus extra for the lamb

½ teaspoon ground cumin

sea salt and freshly ground black pepper

12 oz. lamb steaks, trimmed of fat

7 oz. plum tomatoes, chopped

1 small red onion, thinly sliced into discs

2 tablespoons extra virgin olive oil

1 teaspoon balsamic vinegar

2 whole-wheat pita breads

lemon wedges, to serve

heavy–based stove-top broiler pan or outdoor grill

Serves 2

First make the marinade. Mix together the yogurt, garlic, mint, lemon juice, cumin, salt, and pepper to taste in a bowl. Put the steaks on a plate and smother each piece with the yogurt mix. Cover and leave to marinate in a cool place for a few minutes.

While the lamb is marinating, mix together the tomatoes, red onion, mint sprigs, 1 tablespoon of the olive oil, balsamic vinegar, salt, and pepper to taste.

Remove the lamb from the yogurt marinade. Brush a heavy–based stove-top broiler pan or outdoor grill with the remaining oil and heat until smoking. Cook the lamb for about 3 minutes on each side.

Meanwhile, hold each piece of pita bread briefly under running water and then put it in a toaster or under the preheated broiler for a few minutes. They should puff up but not become brown and crisp. Squeeze lemon juice over the cooked lamb and slice the lamb thickly. Split the pita breads open and fill with the tomato salad and thick slices of lamb.

Variation: The yogurt marinade works well with chicken breast fillets that have been lightly beaten flat before marinating.

Sichuan peppercorns are often used in Chinese cooking to add a woody aroma and peppery flavor. If you can't find them, use Chinese five-spice powder instead. If you don't have time to make a flavored butter, look out for the ready-made garlic and herb ones. Ideally, buy your steaks from a good local butcher.

2 tablespoons flavored butter (see pages 138–139)

2 sirloin or fillet steaks (each weighing about 5 oz.)

1 tablespoon olive oil, plus extra for oiling

1 tablespoon Sichuan peppercorns, crushed

1 teaspoon sea salt flakes

1 ripe avocado, peeled, pitted, and chopped

5 oz. cherry tomatoes, halved

1 small fennel, hard core removed and thinly sliced

3 oz. watercress

2½ oz. bitter salad greens

1 baguette, halved horizontally and across, to serve

For the herb vinaigrette

1 tablespoon white wine or tarragon vinegar

1 tablespoon Dijon mustard

4 tablespoons extra virgin olive oil

1 teaspoon sugar

1 tablespoon chopped fresh tarragon

stove-top broiler pan

Serves 2

peppered steak sandwich
with local market salad

First make the flavored butter of your choice and chill it in the refrigerator until needed.

Lightly score each side of the steaks and rub with the olive oil. Sprinkle the crushed Sichuan peppercorns and salt onto a plate and roll the steaks in the seasoning (if time allows, cover and leave for a while before cooking). Lightly oil a stove-top broiler pan and heat until very hot indeed. Drop each steak directly in the pan. Sear quickly on both sides. Turn the heat down and cook them for about 2–3 minutes on each side, depending on how you like your steak cooked (see below). Cover with foil, and leave to rest for about 5 minutes.

Meanwhile, put the avocado in a large bowl. Add the cherry tomatoes, fennel, watercress, and salad greens. Place all the ingredients for the vinaigrette in a screw-top jar and shake vigorously until evenly combined.

Toss the salad with a little of the herb vinaigrette (any leftover vinaigrette can be stored in the fridge for up to 1 week). Divide the salad between 2 halves of the baguette. Place slices of steak in each and serve immediately.

Cooking steak Rare, medium, or well done? A great tip for testing steak's doneness is to use your face as a guide. Lightly press your (clean) finger onto the surface of the meat. If it feels like your cheek, it's rare; if it feels like your, nose it's medium; if it feels like your forehead, it's well done.

light bites

soups and salads for two

Once everything is peeled and chopped, this country-style chunky soup is surprisingly simple to make. The vegetables are roasted in the oven, which makes their flavor sweet but intense, so all you need to do is throw them in a blender for an instant and nutritious dinner. If you prefer a smoother texture, just push it through a strainer once cooked.

roasted vegetable soup

2 lb. ripe plum tomatoes, halved

1 medium red onion, thinly sliced

2 carrots, peeled and thinly sliced

1 small red chile, left whole

2 garlic cloves, peeled but left whole

a few fresh thyme
or rosemary sprigs

2 tablespoons olive oil

1⅓ cups tomato paste

½ teaspoon sugar

a squeeze of fresh lime juice

sea salt and freshly ground
black pepper

a handful of fresh cilantro,
roughly chopped

a drizzle of extra virgin olive oil and
warm crusty bread, to serve

a roasting pan

Serves 2

Preheat the oven to 400°F.

Put the tomatoes, onions, and carrots in a roasting pan. Add the chile, garlic, thyme or rosemary sprigs, and olive oil and toss until the vegetables are well coated. Place in the preheated oven and roast for about 25 minutes, turning the vegetables occasionally using a large spoon.

Remove from the oven and discard the chile. Blend the roasted vegetables, garlic, and herbs with the tomato purée in a blender or using a hand-held blender. Add the sugar, lime juice, and ⅔ cup cold water, and season well with salt and pepper.

Pour the mixture into a large pan and gently heat through. Add the cilantro just before serving. Ladle into warmed serving bowls and drizzle with a little extra virgin olive oil. Serve immediately with warm crusty bread.

Root vegetable chips make a delicious crunchy topping for this comforting soup, which also works well with pumpkin.

spiced butternut squash and coconut soup

2 tablespoons unsalted butter

1 large white onion, roughly chopped

1 medium carrot, roughly chopped

1 lb. butternut squash, cubed

½ teaspoon ground cumin

1 teaspoon Madras curry paste

1½ cups vegetable stock

1 tablespoon brown sugar

3 tablespoons coconut milk, plus extra to garnish

freshly squeezed juice of ½ lime

sea salt and freshly ground black pepper

a handful of fresh cilantro, chopped

root vegetable chips, to serve

Serves 2–4

Melt the butter in a large saucepan over low heat. Add the onion, carrots, and squash and gently sauté for 5–8 minutes, stirring occasionally, until the vegetables begin to soften. Add the cumin and curry paste and stir over heat for 1 minute until the vegetables are well coated with the spices.

Stir in the stock, sugar, and coconut milk and let simmer for about 20 minutes, or until the vegetables are cooked through and soft.

Blend the soup until smooth, either in a standard blender or using a hand-held blender. Taste, season with salt and pepper, then add the lime juice. Stir in the chopped cilantro. Pour the soup into warmed bowls and swirl some extra coconut milk over the top. Sprinkle with a few root vegetable chips and serve immediately.

These spicy chips make the perfect accompaniment for light dishes such as Chile Scallops (page 93).

spiced sweet potato chips

12 oz. sweet potatoes, peeled and sliced into thin discs

2 tablespoons soy sauce

2 tablespoons olive oil

a handful of fresh cilantro, chopped

sour cream, to serve

a nonstick roasting pan

Serves 4

Preheat the oven to 425°F.

Mix together the oil and soy sauce. Place the sweet potato discs in a nonstick roasting pan in an even, single layer. Pour the oil mixture over the sweet potato and toss the discs until they are coated.

Bake in the preheated oven for 20 minutes, or until golden and cooked through. Serve immediately with sour cream for dipping.

This is a wonderful meal-in-a-bowl that takes only minutes to put together. It is quite spicy, so reduce the quantity of chile if you prefer. Tom yum paste is a treasure to have in your pantry if you have a fondness for Thai food. Use it for stir-fries or Thai curries.

tom yum shrimp noodle soup

4–8 raw jumbo shrimp, shells on
2 tablespoons Thai tom yum paste
1 red chile, seeded and finely chopped
1 bell pepper, thinly sliced
3½ oz. brown cap mushrooms, sliced
3½ oz. leeks, trimmed and thinly sliced
3½ oz. rice noodles
a few fresh cilantro sprigs, to garnish
freshly squeezed juice of 1 lime

Serves 2–4

Peel the shrimp and use a very sharp knife to cut each one along the back so that it opens out like a butterfly, leaving each shrimp joined along the base and at the tail. Remove the black vein.

Bring 2½ cups water to a boil in a large pan. Stir in the tom yum paste until dissolved. Add the chile, bell pepper, mushrooms, and leeks and let the mixture simmer for 5 minutes.

Meanwhile, put the noodles in a large heatproof bowl, cover with boiling water, and leave to sit for 3–5 minutes until just tender before draining in a colander and spooning into deep serving bowls.

Add the shrimp to the tom yum mixture and simmer for a further 2–3 minutes. Pour the tum yum soup over the noodles. Squeeze a little lime juice over each bowl and garnish with a cilantro sprig. Serve immediately.

This oriental rice soup can be enjoyed as a snack at any time, but it's sustaining enough to make a light meal, and it's great if you have a cold. For the best flavor, look out for fresh chicken stock sold in tubs—or better still, when you cook a chicken, make a batch of stock for the freezer.

chicken, lemongrass, ginger, and rice soup

½ cup Thai jasmine or fragrant rice

2 cups chicken stock

1½ tablespoons light soy sauce

½ teaspoon dried red pepper flakes

½ lemongrass stalk, outer leaves removed, finely chopped

thin slice fresh ginger, peeled and finely chopped

2 garlic cloves, thinly sliced

3 boneless chicken breasts (each weighing about 5 oz.), cut into small pieces

1 bell pepper, cored, seeded, and thinly sliced

3 scallions, finely chopped

2 oz. spring greens, finely shredded (optional)

a squeeze of fresh lime juice

freshly ground black pepper

fresh cilantro leaves, to garnish

Serves 2–4

Cook the rice according to the package instructions. Drain, rinse, drain again and set aside until needed.

Heat the stock to the boiling point in a large pan. Add the soy sauce, red pepper flakes, lemongrass, ginger, and garlic, and cook over high heat for 5 minutes.

Add the chicken pieces and bell pepper and let the mixture bubble gently for about 3 minutes, or until the chicken is tender.

Add the cooked rice and cook for a further 1 minute. Finally, stir in the scallions and spring greens (if using). Ladle into warmed bowls. Squeeze a little lime juice over each, season with pepper and garnish with a cilantro leaves. Serve immediately.

Variation: This soup also works well using shelled uncooked shrimp. Simply substitute them for the chicken and cook in the same way. Add a handful of spinach leaves at the end.

This is a great after-work summer salad that could also be served as an accompaniment to grilled chicken or lamb. Marinate the cheese for as long as you like—it will keep in the refrigerator overnight.

Keep the tomatoes out of the fridge—they taste much better and sweeter at room temperature; also, make sure you choose ripe tomatoes and ripe, ready-to-eat avocado.

lemon and herb feta
with tomato and olive salad

5 oz. feta cheese, cut into cubes

1 garlic clove, crushed

2 tablespoons chopped fresh dill

2 tablespoons chopped fresh mint

4 tablespoons extra virgin olive oil

finely grated zest of 1 lemon and freshly squeezed juice of ½ lemon

freshly ground black pepper

warm crusty bread, to serve

For the salad

1 small head of crisp lettuce, roughly chopped

6 oz. ripe plum tomatoes, cut into chunks

1 small cucumber, peeled, seeded, and roughly chopped

2 oz. black kalamata olives, pitted

1 small red onion, thinly sliced

1 ripe avocado, peeled, pitted, and cut into chunks

Serves 2

Put the feta cubes in a shallow bowl. In another small bowl mix together the garlic, herbs, olive oil, and lemon zest and juice. Season the dressing with pepper and pour over the feta. Cover and leave to marinate for a few minutes in a cool place, or in the refrigerator for longer.

Arrange the lettuce leaves in 2 bowls or on 2 plates. Put the tomatoes, cucumber, olives, onion, and avocado on the top, then spoon the marinated feta over the salad. Serve with warm crusty bread.

Pomegranate molasses is a thick, sticky liquid made from reduced pomegranate juice that is used in Middle Eastern cooking. You can buy it from Middle Eastern grocers or "specialty sections" of some supermarkets. It instantly lifts the flavor of summer fruits, duck breasts, and chicken, and is a well-kept secret of many professional kitchens. If you can't get hold of pomegranate molasses, use a good, thick, syrupy balsamic vinegar or reduce a thinner vinegar slowly in a small pan until it has halved in volume.

beet, walnut, and warm goat cheese salad

2 tablespoons pomegranate molasses or reduced balsamic vinegar

1 tablespoon walnut oil

freshly squeezed juice of 1 orange

1 garlic clove, crushed

7 oz. cooked fresh beets, quartered

4 thick slices of ciabatta bread

3½ oz. firm goat cheese, crumbled

3½ oz. mixed salad greens

⅓ cup walnut halves

Serves 2

To make the dressing, mix together the pomegranate molasses or balsamic vinegar, walnut oil, orange juice, and garlic in a bowl, pour over the beets. Cover and leave to marinate in a cool place for 20 minutes.

Preheat the broiler. Lightly toast one side of the ciabatta bread under the broiler. Turn the bread over and arrange the goat cheese on the other side. Grill for a further 3–4 minutes, or until the top begins to turn golden.

Divide the salad greens and walnuts between 2 plates, top with the marinated beet and goat cheese toasts, and pour over the remaining dressing.

This combination of baby spinach, crunchy croûtes, blue cheese, grapes, and pears is a sensation. Italian ciabatta bread makes delicious toasts. Alternatively, you can buy the croûtes ready-made in many supermarkets.

pear, blue cheese, and croûtes salad

For the croûtes

4 oz. ciabatta

2 tablespoons extra virgin olive oil

sea salt and freshly ground black pepper

a few fresh rosemary and thyme sprigs, chopped

For the salad

2 tablespoons Sweet Mustard Dressing (see page 142)

3½ oz. baby spinach leaves

2 oz. Gorgonzola or other firm blue cheese, crumbled

½ cup red seedless grapes, halved

1 ripe pear, cored and sliced

a nonstick baking sheet

Serves 2

Preheat the oven to 400°F.

First make the croûtes. Cut the bread into thin slices and place them on a baking sheet. Drizzle with olive oil and sprinkle with the salt, pepper to taste, rosemary, and thyme.

Place the baking sheet in the preheated oven and bake the croûtes for about 10 minutes, or until the bread is toasted.

Pour the mustard dressing into a large bowl, add the spinach, cheese, grapes, and pear and toss lightly. Pile the dressed salad into serving bowls and top with the croûtes. (You can keep any leftover croûtes in an airtight container for up to 2 weeks; simply refresh in a warm oven before using.)

Variation: You can make this salad more substantial by adding an avocado, cut into chunks, or a few tablespoonfuls of toasted pine nuts.

It is desirable to use only the crunchiest leaves in this salad, but you could, for a change, add some peppery arugula leaves. The salmon has been coated in a ready-made Cajun seasoning, found in the spice section of most supermarkets.

blackened salmon salad

1 clove garlic, halved

3 tablespoons olive oil

2 thick slices of ciabatta, cut into cubes

2 tablespoons Cajun seasoning

1 teaspoon sea salt flakes

2 skinless salmon fillets (each weighing about 5 oz.)

1 head romaine lettuce, washed, dried, and sliced

Parmesan cheese shavings, to serve

For the dressing

1 clove garlic, crushed

⅓ cup good-quality mayonnaise

5 anchovy fillets, finely chopped

freshly ground black pepper

Serves 2

Put the garlic clove halves in a heavy-based frying pan with 2 tablespoons of the olive oil. Heat, then add the bread cubes. Toast over medium heat, tossing frequently, until the cubes are evenly golden brown. Tip them onto a paper towel, discard the garlic, and set aside. Wipe the pan clean.

Mix together the Cajun seasoning and salt on a plate and roll the salmon fillets in the seasoning mix until evenly covered. Place the clean frying pan over high heat and add the remaining oil. When the pan is smoking, add the salmon and cook for 2–3 minutes on each side, until just cooked. Remove from heat and break into rough pieces.

Meanwhile, to make the dressing, put the garlic in the bowl of a food processor or blender along with the mayonnaise and anchovy fillets and process until smooth. Add a few drops of hot water to thin the dressing so that it is the consistency of heavy cream. Season to taste with pepper.

Pour the dressing into a large bowl. Add the romaine leaves and toss well to coat. Arrange the dressed leaves on serving plates. Top with the blackened salmon pieces, garlic croutons, and a sprinkling of Parmesan cheese shavings. Serve immediately.

Here is a tangy chicken salad that can be enjoyed as snack or as part of a larger meal. Pick up a roast chicken on your way home from work and use the freshly roasted warm meat in this unusual and delicious Thai-style salad. The quantities will stretch to make four smaller portions or two more generous ones.

coconut thai chicken salad

2-lb. roast chicken, preferably still warm

¾ cup canned coconut milk

2 tablespoons sweet chili sauce

4 teaspoons Thai fish sauce

freshly squeezed juice of 1 lime

For the salad

1 carrot, peeled and cut into sticks

2 oz. radishes, thinly sliced

1 bell pepper, cored, seeded, and thinly sliced

3 scallions, thinly sliced

1 romaine lettuce, torn into bite-sized pieces

2 tablespoons roasted peanuts or cashew nuts, roughly chopped

handful of a fresh mint leaves

1 lime, quartered

Serves 2–4

Remove the meat from the roast chicken carcass, including the wings and the legs. Tear the meat into bite-sized pieces.

Pour the coconut milk, sweet chili sauce, fish sauce, and lime juice into a bowl and mix well using a fork. Add the chicken meat to the bowl and toss it gently in the coconut dressing until coated.

Put the carrot, radishes, bell pepper, scallions, and lettuce in a bowl and toss to mix, then divide this mixture between serving plates. Arrange the coconut chicken pieces on top and spoon any remaining dressing over the top.

Sprinkle the salads with the chopped peanuts or cashew nuts, garnish with mint leaves, and offer lime quarters for squeezing over. Serve immediately.

Variation: If you want to make the salad more substantial, add rice noodles. Place 5 oz. rice noodles in a large heatproof bowl, cover with boiling water, and leave to sit for 3–5 minutes until just tender before draining in a colander. Toss these with the chicken and coconut dressing and serve on top of the salad.

This is a more sophisticated version of mushrooms on toast. The intense, robust flavor of portobello mushrooms with their lovely meaty juices soaking into thick, crusty toast makes a wonderful week-day dinner. The bacon should be cut into little stubby strips called lardons; these are sold ready-prepared in some supermarkets.

warm mushroom, bacon, and arugula salad

1 tablespoon olive oil

3 slices thick-sliced bacon, cut into lardons (small strips)

4 portobello mushrooms, stems trimmed, caps left whole

1 red onion, chopped into petals

1 garlic clove, crushed

1 tablespoon red wine vinegar or cider vinegar

1 teaspoon brown sugar

sea salt and freshly ground black pepper

1 teaspoon grainy Dijon mustard

4 thick slices of Italian bread, such as ciabatta

2 handfuls arugula, washed and dried

a drizzle of extra virgin olive oil

freshly grated Parmesan cheese, to serve

Serves 2

Heat the olive oil in a frying pan and add the bacon lardons. Stir-fry until golden and crispy. Remove from the pan with a slotted spoon and set aside on a paper towel, leaving the oil and fat in the pan.

Add the mushrooms to the pan along with the onion and garlic, cover, and cook over a moderate heat for about 2 minutes on each side, or until the mushrooms begin to brown. Take the lid off and add the vinegar, sugar, salt and pepper to taste, mustard, and ¼ cup water. Cook until the sugar has dissolved. Return the bacon lardons to the pan and keep warm.

Lightly toast the bread. Put 2 slices on each serving plate. Arrange the arugula on top and drizzle with a little extra virgin olive oil. Place a mushroom on each bed of arugula and spoon the bacon and onion mixture with its pan juices over the top. Sprinkle generously with grated Parmesan cheese and serve immediately.

dinner for friends
impressive yet simple dishes

Your weeknight guests will be delighted with these homemade tartlets. The pastry can be cooked ahead of time and the topping added at the last moment. Frozen puff pastry dough is a great help for cooks with little time to spare. Fresh shavings of Parmesan are best, but Parmesan shavings can also be bought in tubs—another time-saver.

roast plum tomato, goat cheese, and arugula tartlets

2 x 12 oz. packages of frozen puff pastry, defrosted

2 tablespoons extra virgin olive oil

2 tablespoons tomato concentrate

a handful of fresh basil, chopped

6 ripe plum tomatoes

3½ oz. firm goat cheese, crumbled

sea salt and freshly ground black pepper

1 teaspoon sugar

a handful of arugula leaves or watercress

1 oz. Parmesan cheese, shaved

2 heavy-based baking sheets

Serves 4

Preheat the oven to 425°F.

Lightly flour a work surface. Lay out the pastry and cut it into 4 x 6-inch rounds using a small plate as a guide. Prick all over vigorously with a fork and place on a heavy-based baking sheet. Cover with baking parchment and another heavy-based baking sheet. Bake in the preheated oven for about 15–20 minutes, until golden brown. Cooking the pastry this way will ensure that it does not puff up too much but remains crisp. Remove from the oven and set aside.

Preheat the broiler to high. Mix together the olive oil, tomato concentrate and chopped basil. Spread this mixture over the cooked pastry rounds right to the edge. If you have time, peel the tomatoes. To do this, stab a tomato onto the prongs of a fork and plunge into a pan of boiling water, count to 6, then plunge straight into a bowl of cold water to stop the cooking process. The skins should just slip off easily (if the tomatoes are ripe), but if they don't, simply repeat the process.

Slice the tomatoes thinly and arrange them on top of the cooked pastry rounds, making sure they overlap and reach the edges, otherwise the pastry edges will burn. Scatter the cheese over the top, season with salt and pepper and sprinkle over the sugar.

Put the tarts on a baking sheet and place under the preheated broiler to cook until the cheese begins to melt and bubble. Transfer to warmed serving plates and top each tart with some arugula leaves or watercress and Parmesan cheese shavings. Serve immediately.

Variation: You can use other cheeses, such as crumbled Greek feta, sliced mozzarella, cubed Roquefort, or grated Cheddar.

The use of vodka as the poaching liquid transforms this simple salmon dish into a distinctive main course that's ideal for serving to friends. Marinating the fish in the vodka and lime for a full 10 minutes before cooking gives it a lovely citrus flavor.

vodka poached salmon with cilantro pesto

½ cup vodka

finely grated zest and freshly sqeezed juice of 2 limes

4 skinless salmon fillets (each weighing about 8 oz.)

sea salt and freshly ground black pepper

steamed, buttered green beans and mashed potatoes, to serve

For the cilantro pesto

½ cup pine nuts, toasted

a large bunch of fresh cilantro

1 red chile, seeded and roughly chopped

2 garlic cloves

½ cup extra virgin olive oil

2½ oz. Parmesan cheese, finely, freshly grated

3 tablespoons good-quality mayonnaise

Serves 4

Preheat the oven to 375°F.

Pour the vodka into a shallow, non-metallic ovenproof dish and add the lime juice and zest. Put the salmon fillets in the vodka mixture, season well with salt and pepper, cover, and set aside to marinate in a cool place for at least 10 minutes.

Meanwhile, make the cilantro pesto. Put the pine nuts, cilantro, chile, and garlic in the bowl of a food processor. Blitz until evenly chopped, then add the olive oil in a thin stream with the motor running until smooth. Transfer to a bowl and stir in the grated Parmesan cheese and mayonnaise.

Cover the salmon with foil and bake in the preheated oven for 6–7 minutes, or until just tender. Remove the salmon from the oven and discard the poaching liquid. Arrange the salmon fillets on a mound of steamed, buttered green beans with some creamy mashed potatoes and spoon a little of the cilantro pesto over the top. Serve immediately.

The salsa verde that accompanies this tuna steak requires a bit of chopping, but gives the meaty fish a wonderfully intense flavor. You can prepare the potato salad ahead of time and leave it in the dressing, and the salsa verde will keep in the fridge overnight, so all you will need to do at the last minute is to cook the tuna.

tuna steak with warm potato salad and salsa verde

2 tablespoons extra virgin olive oil, plus extra to serve

4–6 fresh tuna steaks (each weighing about 5 oz.)

sea salt and freshly ground black pepper

a few fresh spinach leaves, to serve

For the potato salad

10 oz. baby new potatoes, scrubbed

½ cup extra virgin olive oil

freshly squeezed juice of 1 lemon

2 teaspoons grainy Dijon mustard

2 teaspoons snipped fresh chives

sea salt

For the salsa verde

2 handfuls fresh flat-leaf parsley, chopped

2 tablespoons capers, drained, rinsed, and chopped

4 anchovy fillets, soaked in milk, drained, and finely chopped

3 garlic cloves, crushed

1 oz. green olives, pitted and chopped

⅓ cup extra virgin olive oil

freshly ground black pepper (optional)

Serves 4–6

First make the potato salad. Cook the potatoes in a pan of boiling, salted water until they are just tender, about 15–20 minutes. Meanwhile, pour the olive oil into a medium bowl and add the lemon juice, mustard, and chives. Whisk to form a dressing.

Drain the cooked potatoes and wait until they are cool enough to handle before cutting them into thick slices (or halves if they are very small). Toss them in the dressing until they are thoroughly coated. Set aside.

Combine all the ingredients for the salsa verde in a small bowl and mix well. Taste for seasoning and add a little pepper if needed.

Brush the olive oil over the tuna steaks and season well with salt and pepper. Heat a nonstick frying pan over a high heat until smoking, add the tuna and cook for 2 minutes on each side, turning only once.

Remove from the pan and cut each tuna steak into smaller pieces. Arrange the warm potato salad on each plate and top with the tuna. Spoon the salsa verde over the top. Serve with spinach leaves dressed with a drizzle of extra virgin olive oil.

The accompaniments for this dish need to be cooked in the right order. Start by with the potatoes, then prepare the butter sauce and arrange the trout on the broiler pan. Next cook the onions for the peas and lettuce. When the potatoes are almost cooked, put the trout under the broiler and finish cooking the peas.

broiled rainbow trout with mustard and caper butter

4 fresh trout fillets (each weighing about 5 oz.)

1 tablespoon olive oil

sea salt and freshly ground black pepper

5 tablespoons unsalted butter

freshly squeezed juice of 1 lemon

1 tablespoon small capers, drained and rinsed

1 tablespoon grainy mustard

a bunch of fresh tarragon, chopped

For the pan-fried potatoes

2 lb. new potatoes, scrubbed, and halved if large

2 tablespoons olive oil

2 tablespoons unsalted butter

2 garlic cloves, thinly sliced

sea salt flakes

For the braised peas and lettuce

2 tablespoons unsalted butter

1 onion, finely chopped

2 tablespoons white wine

3 tablespoons crème fraîche

1⅔ cups frozen petits pois

1 small romaine lettuce, shredded

Serves 4

To make the herb butter, melt the butter in a small saucepan over low heat and add the lemon juice, capers, and mustard. Mix to combine and set aside.

Preheat the broiler to medium. Lay the fish on a lightly-oiled broiler pan, skin-side down. Drizzle with the olive oil and season with salt and pepper.

Put the fish under the broiler for about 4 minutes. Carefully remove from the broiler pan and arrange on warmed plates. Add the chopped tarragon to the butter sauce (at the last moment so that it keeps its vibrant green color) and immediately pour the sauce over the trout. Serve with Braised Peas and Lettuce and Pan-fried New Potatoes (see below).

Pan-fried new potatoes Cook the potatoes in a large pan of boiling salted water for about 10 minutes, or until they are just tender. Drain well.

Heat the oil with the butter (if using—it gives the potatoes a better flavor) in a large frying pan and add the hot potatoes. Sauté them over a medium heat, turning frequently until they are evenly golden brown, about 10–15 minutes. Toss the garlic in for the last 2 minutes of cooking. Drain on paper towels, season with salt, and serve while hot and crispy.

Braised peas and lettuce This is a version of the classic peas à la Française. They are a delicious accompaniment to most fish dishes or roast chicken.

Melt the butter in a pan and cook the onion for 2–3 minutes until softened but not colored. Add the white wine and let bubble until the liquid has evaporated. Add the crème fraîche and season. Add the peas and lettuce, cover, and allow to cook for 2–3 minutes until the peas are tender and the cos has wilted. Serve immediately.

This fast, flavorsome dinner is ideal for serving to friends as a light entrée. If you want to reduce preparation time further, you can use two 12-ounce packages of any prepared stir-fry vegetables—such as bell peppers, bean sprouts, and zucchinis—instead of the leeks, carrots, and onion.

Spiced Sweet Potato Chips (see page 64) are a perfect accompaniment. Prepare and cook these first, before you start making the scallop dish, so they will be ready when you are about to serve the scallops, which need to be eaten immediately.

2 tablespoons safflower oil

3 slices thick-sliced bacon, cut into lardons (thin strips)

2 large leeks, trimmed and cut into strips

2 oz. carrots, peeled and cut into strips

1 large onion, thinly sliced

2 red chiles, seeded and thinly chopped

2 garlic cloves, crushed

2 tablespoons honey

2 tablespoons soy sauce

16 large scallops

freshly ground black pepper

Spiced Sweet Potato Chips, to serve

For the lime crème fraîche

⅔ cup crème fraîche

2 tablespoons chopped fresh cilantro, plus extra sprigs to garnish

finely grated zest of 1 lime

1 tablespoon freshly squeezed lime juice

sea salt and freshly ground black pepper

Serves 4

chile scallops with leeks and lime crème fraîche

First make the lime crème fraiche. Put the crème fraîche in a small bowl, add the chopped cilantro and grated lime zest and juice, and season with salt and pepper. Set aside.

Heat 1 tablespoon of the oil in a large nonstick frying pan or wok and stir-fry the bacon lardons until golden. Remove from the pan with a slotted spoon, drain, and set aside on paper towels. In the remaining fat stir-fry the leeks, carrots, onion, chiles, and garlic until soft and golden brown. Add the honey and soy sauce, transfer to a bowl or plate, and keep warm.

Rinse the pan under running water and wipe dry. Add the remaining oil and heat until scorching hot. Season the scallops with pepper and fry briefly on both sides in the pan, allowing around 1½ minutes on each side; they should be firm-textured after cooking. Remove from the pan once they are cooked and keep warm.

Return the vegetable mixture and bacon lardons to the pan and reheat until piping hot. Divide the vegetables between 4 serving plates, top with 4 scallops per plate, and add a generous spoonful of the lime crème fraîche. Garnish each with a cilantro sprig and serve immediately with Spiced Sweet Potato Chips, if desired.

This stunning dish can be prepared even more quickly by using 2 tablespoons of Thai red curry paste instead of the lemongrass, chile, and garlic.

Follow the lead of Belgium—renowned for its Moules Frites—and serve the mussels with French fries. They make a perfect partnership, along with a glass of cold beer. You can use ready-made oven fries, but I would recommend using one of the organic brands.

When serving, put a few large empty bowls on the table for used shells and offer chunks of French bread for mopping up all the delicious juices.

mussels cooked in a creamy lemongrass and lime broth

1¼ cups heavy cream

2 garlic cloves, crushed

2 red chiles, seeded and finely chopped

1 large onion, finely chopped

2 lemongrass stalks, white part only, finely chopped

1 tablespoon Thai fish sauce

5 lb. live mussels, scrubbed and beards removed (throw away any mussels that are open or float to the top ina bowl of cold water)

freshly squeezed juice of 1 lime

a handful of fresh basil leaves, torn

a few fresh cilantro sprigs, to garnish

fries and crusty bread, to serve

Serves 4

Pour the cream into a large pan that has a tight-fitting lid and add the garlic, chiles, onion, lemongrass, and fish sauce. Bring to a boil and let bubble over medium heat for about 8 minutes, or until the onions are soft.

Throw the cleaned mussels into the pan and cover. Cook, gently shaking the pan, for 2 minutes. Uncover and discard any unopened mussels at this stage. Add the lime juice and basil and stir through.

Transfer the cooked mussels to 4 warmed, deep serving bowls and spoon over any remaining sauce. Garnish each one with a cilantro sprig and serve immediately, with fries and plenty of crusty bread.

Serve these scrumptious chicken morsels with a simple tomato and basil salad garnished with black kalamata olives and fresh lemon wedges. It is worth making a double quantity of the goujons and freezing a batch to use another time. Once they have been coated in breadcrumbs, simply open-freeze them on baking sheets, then gather them up into freezer bags. They can be cooked in the oven from frozen for about 15–20 minutes at 400°F.

If you can't find tarragon for the aioli, other green leaf herbs like cilantro or parsley would do very well.

parmesan chicken goujons
with garlic and tarragon aioli

3½ oz. Italian bread, such as ciabatta, roughly chopped

2 oz. Parmesan cheese, finely, freshly grated

freshly ground black pepper

7 tablespoons good-quality mayonnaise

3 skinless, boneless chicken breasts (each weighing about 5 oz.), cut into strips

butter, for greasing

lemon wedges and a tomato, basil, and olive salad, or new potatoes, to serve

For the garlic and tarragon aioli

1 garlic clove, crushed

1 tablespoon chopped fresh tarragon

1 tablespoon extra virgin olive oil

Serves 4

Preheat the broiler to medium or the oven to 400°F.

Put the bread in a food processor and blitz to make breadcrumbs. Tip out onto a large plate, mix in the grated Parmesan cheese, and season with pepper.

Put 3 tablespoons of the mayonnaise in a large bowl and add the chicken strips. Turn in the mayonnaise until they are evenly coated. Lift the strips out and put them on top of the breadcrumb mixture on the plate. Gently toss until each piece is evenly coated.

Meanwhile, make the garlic and tarragon aioli. Mix together the remaining mayonnaise with the garlic, tarragon, and olive oil and season with pepper.

Place the goujons on a greased baking sheet, evenly spaced apart. Cook under the preheated broiler for 4–5 minutes on each side (make sure that the broiler is not too hot or the breadcrumbs will burn). Alternatively, cook them in the preheated oven for 10–15 minutes, turning once, until golden.

When cooked, serve immediately with the garlic and tarragon aioli for dipping, lemon wedges, and a tomato, basil, and olive salad, or, for a more substantial meal, some roasted new potatoes.

The sticky chicken can be prepared ahead of time and refrigerated in a non-metallic dish (being an acidic mixture, it would react with metal). Transfer to a roasting pan just before cooking. In place of Gorgonzola, you could use milder, creamier dolcelatte in the mash.

lemon vinaigrette roasted chicken
with gorgonzola mashed potatoes

2 unwaxed lemons

1 medium onion, finely chopped

2 garlic cloves, halved

6 boneless, corn-fed chicken breasts with skin (each weighing about 6 oz.)

a handful of fresh thyme sprigs

2 tablespoons balsamic vinegar

2 tablespoons sherry or cider vinegar

4 tablespoons honey

⅔ cup olive oil

sea salt and freshly ground black pepper

wilted spinach and steamed or sautéed green beans, to serve

For the gorgonzola mash

3 lb. baking potatoes, peeled and cut into 8 pieces

3 fresh rosemary sprigs (optional)

1 cup milk, warmed

5 tablespoons unsalted butter

4 oz. Gorgonzola cheese, cubed

sea salt

a small roasting tin

Serves 6

Preheat the oven to 425°F.

Grate the zest and squeeze the juice from 1 lemon and set aside. Thinly slice the remaining lemon. Scatter the lemon slices, onions, and garlic over the base of a roasting pan just large enough to hold the chicken breasts comfortably in a single layer. Place the chicken breasts on top of the lemon slices. Season well with salt and pepper and sprinkle with thyme sprigs.

Whisk together the reserved grated lemon zest and juice, vinegars, honey, and olive oil in a bowl. Pour the vinaigrette over the chicken and cook in the preheated oven for 25–30 minutes, or until the chicken is cooked through.

Meanwhile, make the Gorgonzola mash. Rinse the potatoes and cook them in a large pan of boiling salted water with the rosemary sprigs (if using) for 12–15 minutes, or until they start to break up. Drain and mash—you could use a potato ricer or push them through a strainer with the back of a wooden spoon. Put the potato back into the pan. Stir briefly over a low heat so that any excess moisture steams away.

Beat in the warm milk and butter and season well. Stir thoroughly until you have a smooth paste and a peaking consistency—add extra milk if necessary. Gently fold in the Gorgonzola just before you are about to serve so that the cheese is beginning to melt.

Remove the chicken from the oven and then from the tin, and set it aside in a warm place. Place the pan over a medium heat and bubble the juices until syrupy.

To serve, place a large spoonful of mashed potatoes on each warmed plate and put a chicken breast on the top. Spoon over the lemon juices and accompany with wilted spinach and steamed or sautéed green beans.

You can make this tantalizingly spicy dish in less time than you might wait for a take-out delivery. Make sure you have a jar of broiled peppers for the jalfrezi part and look out for good-quality curry pastes in supermarkets and Indian grocers; they cut the time spent grinding or mixing spices. Go for a hot variety containing spices such as chile, cumin, cilantro, tamarind, and turmeric. Serve with Jasmine Rice (see page 46) and pappadoms (wafer-thin Indian breads).

chicken jalfrezi

3 tablespoons vegetable oil

1 onion, roughly chopped

2 garlic cloves, crushed

1 tablespoon hot curry paste

1 tablespoon tomato paste

14-oz can chopped tomatoes (flavored with mixed herbs, if available)

1 teaspoon red wine vinegar

2 broiled red bell peppers, chopped

1 zucchini, diced

1 lb. cooked chicken, cut into bite-size pieces

sea salt and freshly ground black pepper

fresh cilantro sprigs, to garnish

To serve

Jasmine Rice (page 46)

ready-cooked pappadoms

Serves 6

First cook the Jasmine Rice (see page 46). Drain, rinse, and set aside until needed.

Meanwhile, make the curry. Heat the oil in a large frying pan, reduce the heat, and add the onion and garlic. Sauté over medium heat until golden. Add the curry paste and cook for 1 minute to cook off the spices.

Add the tomato paste, chopped tomatoes, vinegar, and a scant cup water to the frying pan. Bring to a boil and simmer, uncovered, for 5 minutes.

Add the broiled bell peppers and diced zucchini and cook for a further 5 minutes until the zucchini are tender. Stir in the chicken pieces and season with salt and pepper. Simmer gently for another 6–7 minutes, or until the chicken is piping hot.

Add the cilantro sprigs at the last moment and serve with the rice and pappadoms.

This is a delicious combination of lamb, tomatoes, mint and butter bean purée. You can make the purée and relish ahead of time and reheat before serving, but cook the lamb chops at the last moment. Serve with a green salad or lightly steamed green vegetables such as broccoli or sugar-snap peas.

rosemary lamb chops with cherry tomato relish and warm butter bean purée

For the butter bean purée

2 tablespoons unsalted butter

1 small onion, finely chopped

2 garlic cloves, crushed

14-oz. can butter beans

3 tablespoons crème fraîche or heavy cream

⅓ cup milk

sea salt and freshly ground black pepper

freshly squeezed juice of 1 lemon, to taste

2 tablespoons chopped fresh parsley

For the tomato relish

2 tablespoons extra virgin olive oil

3 garlic cloves, crushed

1 tablespoon mint jelly

1 tablespoon balsamic vinegar

2½ oz. cherry tomatoes, halved

For the lamb chops

8 lamb chops (weighing about 2 lb. in total)

freshly ground black pepper

5 oz. pancetta or bacon, chopped

4 fresh rosemary sprigs, leaves removed

a shallow roasting pan

Serves 4

Preheat the broiler to high.

First make the butter bean purée. Melt the butter in a frying pan and add the onion and garlic. Stir over a gentle heat for 2 minutes until the onion is soft. Drain the butter beans and add them to the pan with the crème fraîche and milk. Bring to a boil and let bubble for 1–2 minutes. Using a potato masher, lightly crush the bean mixture so that it looks like a rough purée. Taste and season with salt and pepper and lemon juice, and add the chopped parsley. Set aside in a warm place.

To make the tomato relish, whisk together the olive oil, garlic, mint jelly, and vinegar in a bowl. Pour into a small saucepan and add the tomatoes. Lightly warm over low heat for 1–2 minutes.

Season the lamb chops with pepper and place them in a shallow roasting pan. Scatter the pancetta or bacon and the rosemary leaves around the chops. Place under the preheated broiler and cook for 3–4 minutes on each side.

Remove the chops from the pan and leave them to rest in a warm place for 5 minutes. Tip the pancetta or bacon and rosemary with the meat juices into the tomato mixture.

To serve, spoon a tablespoon of the hot butter bean purée onto warmed serving plates and arrange 2 chops per person on the top. Spoon the warm tomato relish over the top and serve immediately.

Since your friends can help themselves and put together their own traditional fajitas, this dish is terrifically straightforward to serve. If you prefer a very spicy guacamole, add a couple of extra jalapeño chiles, seeded and finely chopped.

stir-fried beef fajitas with guacamole and sour cream

4 small sirloin steaks, about 1 inch thick (each weighing about 6 oz.)

4 tablespoons extra virgin olive oil

1 tablespoon pimentón (Spanish oak-smoked paprika)

1 tablespoon cumin

2 ripe Haas avocados, peeled and pitted

freshly squeezed juice of 1 lime

1 small white onion, finely grated

1 large red onion, cut into petals

1 red or green bell pepper, cored, seeded, and thinly sliced

3 garlic cloves, cut into slivers

8–12 wheat or corn flour tortillas

sea salt and freshly ground black pepper

To serve

a handful of arugula leaves

2–3 jalapeño chiles, seeded and chopped

salsa

sour cream

a stovetop grill pan (optional)

Serves 4–6

Preheat the oven to 325°F.

Remove any fat from the beef and cut it diagonally, across the grain, to create finger-length strips. Mix together 2 tablespoons of the olive oil, the pimentón, and cumin in a large bowl. Add the beef pieces and toss until evenly coated in the spiced oil. Set aside while you prepare the guacamole and onions and peppers.

To make the guacamole, roughly mash the avocados in a bowl, leaving some lumps, and stir in the lime juice and white onion. Set aside until needed.

Heat a heavy-based stovetop grill pan or large frying pan over a high heat with the remaining oil and stir-fry the red onion, bell pepper, and garlic for 3–4 minutes, until they start to go limp and the edges begin to char. Remove from the pan and set aside in a warm place.

Wrap the tortillas in foil and place them in the preheated oven to warm, for about 5 minutes. (Alternatively, you can follow the package instructions for warming them in the microwave.)

Meanwhile, wipe the grill pan or frying pan clean with paper towels. Heat until smoking hot, then drop the strips of meat into the pan over high heat, working in batches and turning them frequently. Each batch should take no more than 1–2 minutes to cook. Season the meat with salt and pepper.

To serve, arrange the beef strips, guacamole, bell peppers and onion, arugula, jalapeño chiles, salsa, and sour cream in separate bowls. Wrap the tortillas in a cloth napkin, put them in a basket or dish (so that they don't dry out and get hard), and bring them to the table. Let everyone dig in.

Choose lean pork chops for this dish and trim off any excess fat. The spicy marinade, which makes the chops ideal for broiling, can also be brushed onto chicken breasts and other meats. Begin cooking the potatoes before you cook the pork, but don't add the peas and yogurt until just before serving.

indian grilled pork chops with spiced potatoes and peas

1 tablespoon Madras curry paste

2 tablespoons mango chutney

½ teaspoon ground turmeric

2 tablespoons safflower oil

4 loin pork chops (each weighing about 5 oz.)

5 oz. cherry tomatoes, on the vine if available

sea salt and freshly ground black pepper

For the spiced potatoes and peas

1¾ lb. potatoes, such as Yukon gold, peeled and diced

1 tablespoon safflower oil

2 tablespoons unsalted butter

1 onion, finely chopped

1 garlic clove, crushed

1 teaspoon cumin seeds

1 cup baby peas (fresh or frozen)

2 tablespoons Greek yogurt

sea salt

Serves 4

First make the spiced potatoes and peas. Cook the potatoes for 10 minutes in a pan of boiling salted water. Drain in a colander. Heat the oil and butter in a frying pan and add the onion, garlic, and cumin seeds. Cook over low heat until the onions have softened. Add the potatoes and ½ cup water, and continue to cook until the potatoes are tender, for a further 10 minutes.

Meanwhile, preheat the broiler. Put the curry paste, mango chutney, turmeric, and 1 tablespoon oil in a bowl and mix well. Put the chops on a broiler, season well with salt and pepper, and brush with half the curry mixture. Arrange the cherry tomatoes on the broiler rack alongside the pork and drizzle with the remaining oil.

Cook the chops and tomatoes under the preheated broiler and cook for 5–6 minutes or until the pork is slightly charred. Brush the other side with the remaining curry mixture and cook for a further 5–6 minutes.

Just before you are about to serve, add the peas and yogurt to the potatoes, bring to a boil, and let bubble for 1 minute.

To serve, put a few generous spoonfuls of the spiced potatoes and peas on each warmed serving plate and place a pork chop on top along with some tomatoes, still attached to their vine if possible.

sweet things

delicious treats

quick desserts

Most evenings a bowl of fruit salad, a piece of ripe seasonal fruit, or a square of chocolate is all you need to finish off your meal. But sometimes you need to treat yourself or want to spoil your partner or guests, so these speedy desserts are the solution.

★ Hot Fudge Sauce

Melt 8 oz. good-quality dark chocolate in a pan with ½ cup strong black coffee. Once melted, add 5 tablespoons butter, 4 tablespoons heavy cream, and ½ teaspoon cinnamon. Scoop balls of your favorite vanilla ice cream into a dish, pour over the luscious warm sauce, and dig in! If there are two of you there will be plenty left over for another night. Cover and keep in the fridge.

★ Raspberry Banana Split

Push 1 cup raspberries through a fine-meshed strainer and stir in 1–2 tablespoons of confectioners' sugar to make a sauce. Peel and halve two bananas and put them on serving plates. Add 3–4 scoops of good-quality vanilla or strawberry ice cream, top with a handful of fresh raspberries, and drizzle with the raspberry sauce. Sprinkle with toasted and chopped nuts such as macadamias, almonds, hazelnuts, or peanuts.

★ Champagne Sorbet Cup

This should be reserved for a special occasion or when you really want to impress! In a martini glasses place 2 scoops of good-quality blackberry or mango sorbet. Sprinkle with mixed berries (such as raspberries, strawberries, or blueberries) and slowly and carefully pour a little Champagne or sparkling wine into each glass. Work quickly so that each person receives a sparkling glass.

★ Ice Cream Cookie Sandwich

Mix together 2 tablespoons shredded coconut with 2 tablespoons finely chopped toasted hazelnuts or almonds and put on a small plate. Scoop 4 balls of softened vanilla fudge- or toffee-swirl ice cream onto 4 small chocolate chip cookies. Top with a second cookie and gently press down, pushing the ice cream to the edge. Roll the ice cream in the nut mixture and serve. If making for a crowd, the cookie sandwiches can be made ahead and kept in the freezer. Remove them from the freezer 5 minutes before you want to eat them, to soften.

★ Easy Mango Granita

This is a refreshing and healthy end to a meal. Peel 2 large, ripe mangoes, cut away the flesh, and put it in a food processor or blender. Purée with the juice of 1 lime. Taste and add more juice if necessary. Pour into a shallow freezer-proof dish and freeze overnight. To serve, use a spoon to scrape the frozen mango into "icicle shards" and fill chilled martini glasses. Serve immediately.

★ Strawberry and Passion Fruit Crush

Mash one basket of strawberries with a dash of sugar, then fold in 2 oz. broken ready-made meringue nests and ⅔ cup lightly whipped cream. Spoon into sundae glasses and top with the pulp of 2 passion fruits.

★ Cheat's Chocolate "Tartufo"

Put 2 Heath bars in a freezer bag and bash using the end of a rolling pin until finely crushed. Scoop rich chocolate ice cream into 4 balls and roll in the crushed Heath bars. Place on a baking sheet covered with parchment paper and freeze for 2 hours before serving.

★ Blueberry and Lemon Parfait

Crush 2–3 shortbread cookies into fine crumbs. Mix with 2 tablespoons melted butter. Put half of this mixture in 2 wine glasses. Mix together 2 tablespoons lemon curd with ⅔ cup Greek yogurt, spoon a layer on top of the shortbread mixture, and top with ¼ cup blueberries. Repeat the layers until the glasses are full.

★ Grilled Pineapple with Vodka

Cut off the top and bottom of a large, ripe pineapple and cut off the skin in long thin strips. Use a sharp knife to remove the "eyes." Slice into quarters lengthwise and remove the core. Lay the pineapple onto a baking sheet and drizzle with 6 tablespoons lemon vodka. Season with black pepper. Place under a hot broiler for 5 minutes until golden and serve with lemon sorbet.

★ Simple Summer Berry Brûlée

Divide 1 cup mixed summer berries between 2 shallow serving bowls. Mix together ¼ cup each crème fraîche or sour cream and ricotta with 1½ teaspoon vanilla extract and spoon over the fruits. Sprinkle each with 1 tablespoon soft brown sugar. Leave in the fridge overnight. The sugar magically melts into a caramelized brûlée-style coating.

This is the ultimate in simple desserts—if you have these ingredients in your fridge, freezer, and pantry, you will never be caught out by unexpected guests. The secret is to make sure that the berries are just frozen before pouring over the hot white chocolate sauce. Look out for good-quality white chocolate, which contains cocoa butter; inferior brands will contain vegetable fat.

iced summer berries with hot white chocolate sauce

6 oz. good-quality white chocolate, roughly chopped

⅔ cup whipping cream

1 teaspoon lavender honey

16 oz. frozen mixed berries (such as blueberries, strawberries, raspberries, and blackberries)

Serves 4

Remove the summer berries from the freezer 10 minutes before you want to serve them.

Put the white chocolate, cream, and honey in a heatproof bowl. Bring a large pan of water to a simmer. Place the bowl over the pan, but make sure that the base does not touch the water. Gently heat, stirring continuously with a rubber spatula or wooden spoon, until the chocolate is melted and you have a smooth sauce. Alternatively, you can melt the chocolate with the cream and honey in the microwave. Place them in a small bowl and microwave for a few seconds until smooth. Be careful because white chocolate scorches easily, so don't overcook it.

Arrange the semi-frozen berries on individual serving plates, then pour the hot white chocolate sauce all over the berries so that the heat of the sauce begins to melt and soften them. Serve immediately.

Variation: The hot white chocolate sauce is also delicious spooned over scoops of dark chocolate ice cream or poured over chopped fudge brownies and bananas.

Cranachan is a traditional Scottish dessert marrying oats, whiskey, blackberries, and cream. It is an easy dessert to put together and chill ahead of time if necessary. This recipe also works well with raspberries or with a mixture of blueberries, blackberries, and strawberries. If fresh berries are not in season, excellent bags of frozen mixed berries are always available in the supermarkets.

If you prefer, you can substitute any fruity alcoholic liqueur, such as peach schnapps, Grand Marnier, or Cointreau, for the whiskey.

blackberry cranachan

⅓ cup old-fashioned rolled oats

2 tablespoons soft brown sugar

⅔ cup extra-thick cream

2 tablespoons whiskey, plus extra for drizzling (optional)

1 pint blackberries

a baking sheet

Serves 2

Preheat the broiler.

Mix the oats and sugar together and spread them out on a baking sheet. Place the sheet under the preheated broiler. Cook until the sugar is caramelized, stirring the mixture from time to time. Remove from the broiler and set aside to cool.

Pour the cream into a large bowl, add the whiskey, and stir until smooth. Loosely break up the cooled oat mixture between your fingers and add most of the crunchy oats to the cream, reserving a few tablespoons for the top.

Place some of the berries in the bottom of 2 large wine glasses. Spoon a dollop of the cream over the top and then repeat the layers of fruit and cream a second time, finishing with the remaining blackberries.

To finish, sprinkle over the reserved oat mixture and drizzle with a little more whiskey, if required. Serve immediately.

This is a grown-up version of baked bananas, flavored with warm spices and a little citrus. Bananas are best eaten and cooked when slightly green, firm, and just ripe—don't use a banana for cooking if the skin has become speckled.

The rich homemade coconut ice cream is a breeze to make as it doesn't need any churning or beating during freezing. It can be made the day beforehand and frozen overnight. But, if you don't have time to make the ice cream, simply add a dash of Cointreau or coconut liqueur to some lightly whipped or thick cream.

3 cardamom pods

freshly squeezed juice of 1 orange and 1 lime

3 tablespoons soft brown sugar

6 black peppercorns

2 tablespoons unsalted butter

2 tablespoons Cointreau, rum, or brandy

4 ripe bananas, peeled

For the easy coconut ice cream

2 egg yolks

¼ cup confectioners' sugar

1 cup (8 oz.) mascarpone cheese

2 teaspoons real vanilla extract

2 tablespoons coconut liqueur, such as Malibu

a shallow ovenproof dish

Serves 4

boozy bananas with easy coconut ice cream

Preheat the broiler to high.

Remove the cardamom seeds from the pods and crush them using a pestle and mortar (or put the seeds in a plastic bag and crush with a rolling pin). Put the crushed seeds in a pan with the orange and lime juices, brown sugar, peppercorns, butter, and Cointreau, rum, or brandy. Warm gently over low heat until the butter has melted.

Quarter the bananas lengthwise and put them in a shallow ovenproof dish with the juice mixture. Place the dish under the preheated broiler until they begin to turn golden brown, about 5–7 minutes.

Serve the bananas whilst still warm with Easy Coconut Ice Cream (below).

Easy Coconut Ice Cream Put the egg yolks in a large bowl with the confectioners' sugar. Beat with an electric whisk for about 2 minutes or until thickened and light in color. Whisk in the mascarpone, vanilla extract, and coconut liqueur. Scrape into a freezerproof container and freeze for at least 6 hours or overnight. Place in the fridge to soften 10 minutes before serving.

Variation: This ice cream also goes well with a tropical fruit salad made from mango, paw paw, lychees, and passion fruit.

This has the same sticky toffee sauce that is traditionally used in the famous sponge dessert, but in this recipe the tartness and spiciness of the apples cuts through the sweet, buttery toffee sauce. Sticky toffee sauce is very versatile and can be served with ice cream or spooned over other baked fruit, such as bananas, pears, peaches, or apricots. The apples can be prepared in the morning and popped into the oven as soon as you get home.

baked apples with dates and sticky toffee sauce

For the sticky toffee sauce

5 tablespoons unsalted butter

⅓ cup soft dark brown sugar

5 tablespoons heavy cream

For the stuffed apples

⅓ cup dried dates, roughly chopped

½ oz stem ginger in syrup, drained and finely chopped

2 tablespoons walnuts or pecan nuts, roughly chopped

4 large cooking apples, such as Granny Smith or Courtland, cored

cream or good-quality vanilla ice cream, to serve

a medium ovenproof dish or roasting pan

Serves 4

Preheat the oven to 300°F.

First make the sticky toffee sauce. Put the butter, sugar, and cream in a pan over low heat. Bring to a boil and cook for 1 minute. Remove from the heat and set aside.

Mix together the dates, ginger, and walnuts or pecan nuts. Stuff half this mixture into the cored apples and stir the remainder into the toffee sauce.

Arrange the stuffed apples in an ovenproof dish or roasting pan so that they fit tightly. Pour the toffee sauce over the apples and cover the entire pan with aluminum foil.

Bake in the preheated oven for 25–30 minutes, basting the apples with the sauce occasionally. Remove the pan from the oven and allow the apples to cool for 2 minutes. Serve while still warm, with pouring cream or vanilla ice cream.

These ripe, luscious figs poached in the mellow distinctive flavor of Marsala and served with creamy ricotta cheese are hard to beat. If figs aren't available, you can use ripe peaches or plums, but they will need an extra 5–10 minutes' cooking time. Italian ricotta cheese is a fresh, soft, snowy white cheese with a mild, slightly sweet flavor. You can cook this pudding ahead of time and either reheat it in a low oven or serve it at room temperature.

roast figs with honey and marsala

3 tablespoons Tupelo or orange blossom honey

2 tablespoons unsalted butter, melted

1 teaspoon ground cinnamon

3 tablespoons Italian Marsala wine or sweet dessert wine

8 large, ripe figs

½ cup ricotta cheese, to serve

an ovenproof dish

Serves 4

Preheat the oven to 400°F.

Put the honey, butter, cinnamon, and Marsala or dessert wine in a small pan. Heat gently over low heat and bring to a boil. Let it bubble for 1–2 minutes, until slightly thickened.

Using a small, sharp knife, make a ½-inch deep, star-shaped cut in the top of each of the figs. Gently squeeze the bases with your fingers to open each fruit up like a flower.

Arrange the figs upright in an ovenproof dish so that they fit tightly and pour the wine mixture over each fig. Cook in the preheated oven for about 8–10 minutes, or until slightly blackened on the tips and golden.

Lift the figs onto serving plates and add a large dollop of ricotta. Spoon the deliciously syrupy juices over the top. Serve immediately.

You will find that most Italians have their own versions. This quick and easy recipe is a winner when you've got friends coming over for dinner straight after work, as it can be assembled in the morning and left in the fridge to improve during the day. I always keep a package of ladyfingers biscuits in the pantry and a tub of mascarpone in the fridge. A strong black espresso coffee made from freshly ground beans will give you a more intense and authentic flavor, but you can use an instant coffee (made fairly strong), if preferred.

raspberry and ginger tiramisù

5 oz. raspberries

2 teaspoons sugar

8 ladyfingers

½ cup cooled strong black coffee, such as espresso

⅓ cup coffee-flavored liqueur, such as Tia Maria or Kahlúa, or a cream liqueur, such as Baileys

8 oz. mascarpone cheese

¼ cup confectioners' sugar

1 teaspoon ground ginger

1 tablespoon milk

cocoa powder, for dusting

a few pinches of ground cinnamon

4 sundae dishes, martini glasses, or wine glasses

Serves 4

Put the raspberries in a bowl, add the sugar and lightly mash with a fork to dissolve the sugar. Spoon the fruit into 4 glass sundae dishes, martini glasses, or large wine glasses.

Pour the coffee and coffee or cream liqueur into a small bowl and mix together. Dip both ends of the ladyfingers in the coffee mixture so that they absorb the liquid and darken in color, then put them on top of the raspberries. Use your fingers to press the ladyfingers down a little to fit the glass.

Put the mascarpone, confectioners' sugar, and ginger in a large bowl and beat to combine. Gradually beat in the milk to form a smooth, creamy mixture. Spoon this mixture over the ladyfingers. Dust with a little cocoa powder and sprinkle a pinch of cinnamon over each glass.

Serve immediately or refrigerate until ready to serve.

Variation: You could use amaretti biscuits instead of the ladyfingers. They give the dessert a lovely almond flavor.

These heavenly little chocolate pots are so rich and silky, you only need to serve a small amount, but if you want to serve a more generous portion, simply double the ingredients. They are particularly delicious served with a tiny scoop of orange or strawberry sorbet on the top (use a melon baller rather than an ice cream scoop to make these). You could also serve the pots with some strawberries or redcurrants and a little shortbread or *langue du chat* biscuits on the side. Ideally, make them the night before you are serving them as they need a few hours to set in the fridge.

quick chocolate pots

1 egg

⅓ cup unsweetened cocoa powder

3 tablespoons sugar

4 tablespoons unsalted butter, softened

½ teaspoon pure vanilla extract

⅓ cup whole milk

4 espresso or demitasse cups

Serves 4

Put the egg, cocoa powder, sugar, butter, and vanilla extract in a food processor or blender. Blend until smooth. Pour the milk into a small pan and gradually bring to a boil.

Add the hot milk to the ingredients in the food processor or blender and blend on high speed until smooth. Pour the mixture into 4 tiny espresso or demitasse cups. Cover with plastic wrap and put in the fridge to chill until set, 4–5 hours. Remember to take them out of the fridge a good 20 minutes before you want to eat them as the chill will spoil their silky texture.

Variations: Instead of vanilla, try these other flavors, which can be added to the milk for a subtle difference; orange zest or orange flower water, rose extract, or add a fresh mint sprig to the milk before bringing it to the boil and strain before adding to the other ingredients.

These very indulgent and very chocolatey individual baked sponges are self-saucing. The option of a hazelnut and chocolate topping makes them extra special and very popular with chocoholics! Serve the puddings straight from the oven as the sponge quickly absorbs the sauce.

warm chocolate puddings

For the chocolate sauce

¼ cup unsweetened cocoa powder

2½ cups soft brown sugar

For the chocolate pudding

1 cup all-purpose flour

a pinch of salt

2 teaspoons baking powder

⅓ cup unsweetened cocoa powder

1 cup whole milk

5 tablespoons unsalted butter, melted

½ cup plus 1 tablespoon sugar

2 large eggs

1 teaspoon real vanilla extract

créme fraîche, mascarpone cheese, or vanilla ice cream, to serve

For the hazelnut topping (optional)

6 tablespoons light cream

2 tablespoons brown sugar

2 oz. best-quality dark chocolate, finely chopped

½ cup chocolate and hazelnut spread, such as Nutella

4 x 5-oz. ramekins

Serves 4

Preheat the oven to 350°F.

First make the chocolate sauce. Pour a scant cup boiling water into a small saucepan, add the cocoa powder and brown sugar, and lightly whisk over a low heat making sure that there are no lumps and the sugar has dissolved. Transfer the batter to a jug then pour into four dishes or ramekins.

To make the puddings, sift the flour with the salt, baking powder, and cocoa powder into a large bowl. Whisk in the milk, melted butter, sugar, eggs, and vanilla extract until a thick, smooth batter forms. Transfer the batter to a jug, then pour it into the ramekins so that the mixture comes halfway up the sides. Place the ramekins on a baking sheet.

Pour the chocolate sauce mixture carefully over the prepared puddings and bake in the preheated oven for 15–20 minutes; they should still be wobbly in the center when they are ready.

While the puddings are cooking make the hazelnut topping (if using). Put the cream and brown sugar in a small saucepan, bring to a boil, then remove the pan from the heat. Add the chopped chocolate and stir until melted. Add the Nutella and stir until smooth.

Top each pudding with a dollop of créme fraîche, mascarpone, or a scoop of vanilla ice cream and offer the hazelnut topping in a warm jug for pouring (if using).

Using fresh lavender in this recipe gives the shortcakes an exquisite flavor. If you can't find any, substitute a drop or two of rosewater or orange flower water. The recipe makes about 20 biscuits. They will keep in an airtight container for up to a week and are great for offering to friends who pop in for coffee. They also freeze well, so make up a batch and keep any that are left over to make a speedy and impressive dessert any time.

We have used heart-shaped cutters here, but round, star or crescent shapes would also work well.

lavender shortcake hearts
with raspberries and lemon curd cream

For the shortcake hearts

3 lavender heads, flowers removed

¼ cup confectioners' sugar, plus extra for dusting

8 tablespoons unsalted butter, softened

⅔ cup all-purpose flour

⅓ cup cornstarch

For the lemon curd cream

¼ cup prepared lemon curd

½ cup heavy cream, whipped

1 cup fresh raspberries

Serves 4

Preheat the oven to 300°F.

To make the biscuits, put the lavender flowers and confectioners' sugar in a food processor and blitz until the lavender is powdered. Add the butter and process for 1 minute. Add the flour and cornstarch and process until the mixture begins to come together to form a soft dough. Wrap and chill in the fridge for 30 minutes.

Lightly flour a work surface and tip the dough out onto it. Gently knead the dough with your hands to bring it together, then roll out thinly.

Use a heart-shaped biscuit cutter to cut out shapes—you will need 8 to serve 4 people. Place the biscuits on a baking sheet lined with baking parchment and bake in the preheated oven for 10–12 minutes, or until pale golden and set. Remove from the oven and cool on a wire rack.

To make the filling, gently fold the lemon curd into the whipped cream. To assemble, place a little of the cream in the center of a shortbread, arrange a quarter of the raspberries over the top, place a biscuit on the top at an angle, and dust with confectioners' sugar. Serve immediately.

I use sweet eating apples in this recipe as they keep their shape, unlike cooking apples which result in a rather wet and mushy cake.

If you are using the standard size of ramekin (½ cup) this recipe will serve six, but if you have the larger 1-cup capacity ramekins it will serve four. The cakes can be cooked ahead of time, but leave them in the pan and reheat them in a warm oven before turning out and serving.

upside-down apple cakes

12 tablespoons unsalted butter, plus extra for greasing

½ cup light brown sugar

2 dessert apples, such as Braeburn or Golden Delicious, peeled, cored, and roughly chopped

finely grated zest of ½ lemon

½ teaspoon ground nutmeg

½ teaspoon ground cinnamon

12 walnut halves

½ cup plus 1 tablespoon granulated sugar

1 scant cup self-rising flour

1 teaspoon baking powder

2 eggs

For the ginger cream:

¼ cup crème fraîche or sour cream

2 pieces of stem ginger in syrup, drained and finely chopped

1 teaspoon of syrup from the stem ginger

6 x ½-cup or 4 x 1-cup ramekins

Serves 4–6

Preheat the oven to 350°F. Lightly grease 6 ½-cup or 4 1-cup ramekins.

Put the brown sugar and 4 tablespoons of the butter in a heavy-based saucepan with 2 tablespoons water and heat until melted. Gradually bring to a boil and cook for about 1 minute, or until caramelized. Spoon 1 tablespoon of the caramel sauce into the base of each prepared ramekin. Set aside the remaining sauce.

Put the chopped apples, lemon zest, nutmeg, cinnamon, and walnuts in a large bowl and mix to combine. Divide the mixture between the ramekins.

To make the sponge, put the remaining butter, granulated sugar, flour, and baking powder in the bowl of a food processor and blend for a couple of seconds before adding the eggs. Blitz for a further 10–15 seconds, then stop as soon as the mixture comes together.

Spoon the cake mixture into the ramekins. Place them on a baking sheet and cook in the preheated oven for 15–20 minutes, or until the sponge bounces back when lightly touched. Meanwhile, to make the ginger cream, mix together the crème fraîche, stem ginger, and ginger syrup. Remove the cakes from the oven and run a knife around the edges. Leave to sit for 5 minutes before inverting onto warmed serving plates.

To serve, gently reheat the reserved caramel sauce and spoon over the apple cakes. Serve immediately, topped with a spoonful of ginger cream.

Having a packet of puff pastry in the freezer is always a great standby for an instant fruit tart. You can use practically any fruit; peaches, nectarines, apricots, plums, apples, blueberries, pineapple, or a mixture of berries.

Cinnamon will go with most fruits, or you could try seasoning plums with mace or apricots with nutmeg. Flaked almonds, walnuts, or pecan nuts would also be good added to the fruits.

To crush sugar cubes, put them in a plastic freezer bag and lightly beat with the end of a rolling pin. They will give a delicious crunchy effect.

individual caramelized
pear and cranberry tarts

1 13 oz.-sheet frozen puff pastry, defrosted

2 large ripe pears, peeled, halved, and cored

¼ cup dried cranberries

2 tablespoons unsalted butter, chilled and diced

milk, to glaze

3 tablespoons sugar

1 teaspoon ground cinnamon

light cream, to serve

a nonstick baking sheet

Serve 4

Preheat the oven to 425°F. Put a nonstick baking sheet in the oven to heat.

Lightly flour a work surface and unroll the pastry. Flatten it out onto the work surface and use a sharp knife or a pizza wheel to cut it into 4 squares.

Place a pear half in the center of each pastry square and divide the dried cranberries between the squares. Scatter with the diced butter. Brush the edges with a little milk. Mix the granulated sugar or crushed sugar cubes with the cinnamon and sprinkle over the top.

Carefully slide the tarts onto the hot baking sheet and return to the preheated oven to cook for about 35–40 minutes, or until the pastry is golden brown and crisp and the pears are tender. Serve whilst still warm with light cream for pouring.

transforming simple food

sauces and dressings

There are plenty of bottled sauces, dressings, marinades, and rubs available in the supermarkets, but they are expensive and will never taste as good as their home-made equivalents.

The easy, yet imaginative, recipes in this chapter are ideal for the busy person who wants to prepare delicious food fast. Become a creative cook by understanding how a few magic ingredients can transform simple food into something that both tastes and looks amazing. Spend a little time at the weekend making up a batch of pestos and butters, store them in your fridge or freezer and you are all set to rustle up a delicious week-night supper, bursting with fresh flavors, in no time at all. All you need do is boil some pasta, broil a piece of fish, or assemble a simple salad and add your magic ingredient. An invaluable piece of equipment, for most of these recipes, is a mini food processor.

home-made pestos

Everything about a home-made pesto is better than a pesto from a jar, from the color to the smell—not to mention the taste! Pestos are perfect for stirring into cooked pasta, spreading on pizzas, or using as a topping for broiled fish or chicken. Put the pestos in a screw-top jar, add a thin layer of oil, and store them in the fridge for up to a week. They will also freeze well.

mint, ginger, and almond pesto

This is lovely spooned over grilled fish or barbecued vegetables, added to clear vegetable soup, or tossed into cooked noodles. Toasting the almonds gives the pesto a more intense flavor. Toast the almonds in the oven for 5–6 minutes at 400°F, making sure you keep an eye on them as they burn quickly.

1-inch piece fresh ginger, peeled and grated
a handful fresh mint leaves
½ cup vegetable oil
2 tablespoons light soy sauce
1 tablespoon freshly squeezed lime juice
1 garlic clove, crushed
⅔ cup almonds, toasted

Put all the ingredients in the bowl of a mini food processor and blitz until smooth.

cilantro, chile, and peanut pesto

This hot and spicy pesto is perfect with vegetable and shrimp stir-fries, stirred through pasta or noodles, and served as a dip for crudités.

⅔ cup roasted and salted peanuts
1 garlic clove, crushed
1 small hot chile, seeded and chopped
a handful of fresh cilantro
finely grated zest of 1 lime
½ cup peanut or safflower oil
sea salt and freshly ground black pepper

Put the peanuts, garlic, and chile in the bowl of a mini food processor. Blend, then add the cilantro and lime zest, season generously, and pulse to form a course mix. Allow the motor to run and then, in a steady flow, add the oil to form a smooth paste. Taste and season as necessary.

bell pepper and walnut pesto

Serve this warm as a dip for crudités, stirred into cooked pasta, spooned over grilled halloumi cheese, or as a sauce with grilled lamb or steak.

2 grilled red peppers
⅓ cup walnut pieces, toasted
3 scallions, chopped
1 garlic clove, crushed
2 tablespoons chopped fresh parsley
4–5 tablespoons extra virgin olive oil
sea salt and freshly ground black pepper

Put all the ingredients in a mini food processor and blitz until smooth. Taste and season as necessary.

Variation: If you have time, roast your own red peppers; place under a hot broiler until the skins are blackened on all sides. Remove and put in a plastic bag for 10 minutes, then slip off the skins.

Other quick ideas for pesto:

★ Swirl a tablespoonful of pesto into vegetable soup to add extra flavor and color.

★ Spread on a chicken or ham sandwich instead of mayonnaise.

★ Spread on a toasted bread and top with sliced tomatoes, a drizzle of olive oil, and some freshly ground black pepper.

★ Use to perk up dressings, mayonnaise, or sour cream dressing.

★ Use in place of a tomato sauce on a home-made pizza.

★ Dollop onto baked potatoes or omelets.

★ Add a dash of pesto to canned tomato soup to bring it back to life.

artichoke and almond pesto

This has a lovely creamy texture and subtle flavor. Add to pasta or spread onto warm ciabatta toasts, or serve as a dip with bread sticks. Marinated artichoke hearts can be found loose at deli counters or in jars in the Italian section of supermarkets.

4–6 roasted and marinated artichokes hearts, drained

⅔ cup almonds, toasted

2 tablespoons chopped fresh basil

1 garlic clove, crushed

4 tablespoons extra virgin olive oil

1 oz. Parmesan cheese, finely, freshly grated

sea salt and freshly ground black pepper

Put the artichokes, almonds, basil, and garlic in a mini food processor. Blitz until the mixture looks like coarse meal. Add the oil in a thin stream with the motor running to form a smooth paste. Transfer the purée to a bowl and stir in the Parmesan cheese. Taste and season as necessary.

broccoli, parmesan, and basil pesto

This is a wonderfully vibrant green pesto and is delicious tossed through pasta, spread onto toast, or served as a warm dip.

4 oz. broccoli florets

1 oz. pine nuts, toasted

1 large garlic clove, crushed

1 red chile, seeded and finely chopped

3 tablespoons extra virgin olive oil

2 oz. Parmesan cheese, finely, freshly grated

freshly squeezed juice of ½ lemon

sea salt and freshly ground black pepper

Cook the broccoli in a pan of boiling salted water until tender about 6–7 minutes. Drain. Meanwhile, put the pine nuts, garlic, and chile in a mini food processor and pulse to form a coarse mix. Add the broccoli and olive oil and pulse until the mixture is smooth, then add the Parmesan cheese and lemon juice and pulse again. Taste and season as necessary.

classic basil pesto

A lot of precious leaves are needed to make up this sauce, but it is well worth the indulgence. Serve with pasta, spread on toasts and pizza, or add to mashed potatoes and soups.

1 cup fresh basil leaves

1 large garlic clove, crushed

1 oz. pine nuts, toasted

5–6 tablespoons extra virgin olive oil

a pinch of sea salt

1 oz. Parmesan or Pecorino Romano cheese, finely, freshly grated

Put the basil, garlic, pine nuts, olive oil, and salt in a mini food processor. Blend until smooth, then stir in the grated cheese.

flavored butters

Flavored butters are quick and easy to make and can transform otherwise plain food in an instant. If you have a microwave, the butters can be softened for about 15 seconds and the flavorings beaten into the butter in a bowl. Alternatively, you can simply combine all of the ingredients in a mini food processor.

lemon and basil butter

This has a lovely fresh and zingy flavor. Melt over steamed asparagus and broccoli, or serve with baked or grilled fish. Use instead of plain butter in a smoked salmon sandwich.

8 tablespoons unsalted butter, softened
1 teaspoon finely grated lemon zest
1 tablespoon finely chopped fresh basil
freshly ground black pepper
2 tablespoons freshly squeezed lemon juice

Put the softened butter, lemon zest, and basil in a bowl and season with pepper. Beat until smooth, adding the lemon juice gradually and beating after each addition. Scoop the prepared butter out onto a large piece of waxed paper or plastic wrap and shape into a log about 5 inches in length, wrap well, and twist each end. Chill in the fridge for at least 25–30 minutes or until firm. Cut the butter into handy ⅜-inch slices. Store in an airtight container in the fridge for up to 2 weeks or bag up, label, and freeze for up to 1 month.

tarragon and mustard butter

This butter works well with steak, tuna, or salmon, grilled chicken or duck breasts or home-made burgers. It even makes Brussels sprouts a joy! Blanching the tarragon in boiling water keeps the leaves a brilliant green and enhances the flavor, but it's not essential to do this.

3 tarragon sprigs, leaves removed
8 tablespoons unsalted butter, softened
2 tablespoons grainy Dijon mustard
sea salt and freshly ground black pepper

Cook the tarragon leaves in a pan of boiling salted water for 2 minutes, drain, and rinse under cold running water, then dry thoroughly. Put the softened butter, blanched tarragon, mustard, and pepper to taste in a bowl and beat until smooth. Follow method for chilling as for Lemon and Basil Butter (left).

moroccan spiced butter

This is a great instant butter as all the dry ingredients are likely to be in your pantry. It works well with grilled lamb chops or grilled eggplant and zucchini. Crushing the whole spices really brings out the flavors and essential oils, but you can use ground coriander and cumin, if easier.

1 teaspoon dried red pepper flakes
1 teaspoon coriander seeds
1 teaspoon cumin seeds
½ teaspoon sea salt flakes
8 tablespoons unsalted butter, softened

Put the spices and salt in a mortar and crush lightly with a pestle. Alternatively, put the spices and salt in a heavy bowl and grind using a sturdy wooden spoon. Beat the seasoning mix into the softened butter in a bowl until evenly combined. Follow method for chilling as for Lemon and Basil Butter (far left).

Quick ideas for flavored butters:

★ Spread onto bread rolls, use as part of a sandwich filling or smear onto hot toast for a quick and tasty snack.

★ Add extra taste to steamed vegetables, corn-on-the-cob, or baked potatoes.

★ Melt over grilled meats or use as a seasoning on plain grilled steaks, pork chops, or lamb steaks.

★ With chicken—use your fingers to push the butter under the skin of chicken breasts before oven-baking them.

★ With fish—smear over fish fillets before grilling, use to pan-fry a fillet of fish, or serve melting over a bowl of mussels.

★ Add to gravies and sauces to invigorate and enrich the flavor.

gorgonzola and garlic butter

This goes magnificently with steak. Tuck slices of butter between steak halves and top with another butter slice just before serving. It also works well with pork chops or smeared under the skin of chicken breasts before baking them in the oven.

8 tablespoons unsalted butter, softened

2 garlic cloves, crushed

2½ oz. Gorgonzola, or other firm blue cheese, such as Stilton, crumbled

2 tablespoons finely chopped fresh parsley

Put the softened butter in a bowl with the crushed garlic, blue cheese, and chopped parsley, and beat until evenly combined. Follow method for chilling as for Lemon and Basil Butter (see facing page).

anchovy and caper butter

Smother on grilled fish fillets, such as salmon, mackerel, or haddock, or spread onto hot toast and top with arugula leaves.

2 garlic cloves, crushed

5 anchovy fillets, soaked in milk for 10 minutes and drained

2 tablespoons capers, drained and rinsed

1 tablespoon chopped fresh parsley

a squeeze of lemon juice

8 tablespoons unsalted butter, softened

freshly ground black pepper

Put the garlic, drained anchovy fillets, capers, parsley, and lemon juice in the bowl of a mini food processor. Blend until smooth. Add the butter and blitz until evenly combined. Season with pepper. Follow method for chilling as for Lemon and Basil Butter (see facing page).

hot paprika butter

Spanish oak-smoked paprika (hot pimentón) is not like the relatively bland paprika spice that we are used to. It has a strong hickory-smoked flavor and is often used to season Tex-mex pork, beef, and lamb casseroles. This incredibly speedy butter is delicious served with grilled steaks or chicken breasts, or melted in a baked potato.

8 tablespoons unsalted butter, softened

2 teaspoons hot pimentón (Spanish oak-smoked paprika)

Put the softened butter in a bowl with the paprika and beat until evenly combined. Follow method for chilling as for Lemon and Basil Butter (see facing page).

marinades and spice rubs

Marinades tenderize and add flavor to meat and also add a bit of zing to fish and vegetables. Spice rubs are generally used to season raw meat and fish, but they can also be mixed with butters and oils. Make rubs in big batches as they will keep for about two months in screw-top jars, if stored in a cool, dark place.

soy, honey, and chili marinade

This spicy Thai marinade is great for tossing into shrimp before grilling, or brushing onto chicken breasts before oven-baking or stirring into strips of pork before stir-frying.

2 tablespoons soy sauce

1 tablespoon honey

2 teaspoons Thai fish sauce

2 tablespoons sweet chili sauce

Put all the ingredients together in a small bowl and whisk until evenly combined.

Place the food you are marinating in a shallow, nonreactive dish. Pour the marinade into the dish and turn the food once to make sure it's coated. If you can, cover and let it marinate for about 30 minutes in a cool place. When ready to cook, remove from the marinade and cook as intended.

tex-mex marinade

This is a "hickory" marinade for spare ribs or chicken drumsticks. It's also a great sauce to serve with hamburgers from the grill.

2 tablespoons tomato ketchup

1 garlic clove, crushed

1 cup tomato paste

1 tablespoon red wine vinegar or balsamic vinegar

1 tablespoon Worcestershire sauce

2 teaspoons Tabasco sauce

½ teaspoon pimentón (Spanish oak-smoked paprika)

2 tablespoons chopped fresh cilantro

freshly squeezed juice of ½ lime

Put the ketchup, garlic, tomato paste, vinegar, Worcestershire sauce, Tabasco, paprika, and 1 cup boiling water in a pan. Cover and simmer for 10 minutes. If using as a marinade (see left), set aside to cool. If using as a sauce, stir in the cilantro and lime juice just before serving.

greek lemon and herb marinade

This marinade uses three classic Greek ingredients—olive oil, lemon, and oregano. It can be used to marinate vegetables, meat, or fish and also as a basting sauce when cooking chicken. It is lovely drizzled over grilled haloumi cheese or a feta, olive, tomato, and onion salad.

finely grated zest and freshly squeezed juice of 1 lemon

1 tablespoon chopped fresh oregano

1 teaspoon freshly ground black pepper

1 teaspoon sea salt flakes

⅓ cup extra virgin olive oil

Put the zest in a mortar or heavy mixing bowl and add the oregano, pepper, and salt. Grind with a pestle or sturdy wooden spoon to release the essential oils in the lemon and oregano. Whisk in the lemon juice and olive oil in a steady stream with a wire whisk. To use, follow method for Soy, Honey, and Chili Marinade (far left).

More easy marinades and rubs:

★ **Plum and soy** Mix 4 tablespoons plum sauce with 2 tablespoons soy sauce. Good for brushing onto pork chops, spareribs, duck breasts, or chicken breasts

★ **Marmalade and ginger** Mix 4 tablespoons thick-cut marmalade with 1 tablespoon sweet chili sauce, 1 teaspoon soy sauce, and 1 tablespoon peeled and finely grated fresh ginger root to make a sticky marinade that's good with chicken breasts, duck breasts, and pork and lamb chops.

★ **Chinese Five Spice** Mix together 2 tablespoons soy sauce, ½ teaspoon Chinese five-spice powder, ½ teaspoon runny honey, ½ teaspoon garlic powder, and 2 tablespoons sesame or peanut oil. Great for marinating fish or adding to vegetable stir-fries.

mustard and herb rub

This is good for rubbing onto pork chops or smearing onto the trimmed fat of a rack of lamb. Or try massaging into chicken breasts and steaks.

2 tablespoons Dijon mustard
1 tablespoon chopped fresh flat leaf parsely
2 teaspoons chopped mint
2 teaspoons chopped chives
freshly ground black pepper

In a bowl mix the mustard with the fresh herbs and season with black pepper. Store in a dry screw-top glass jar until required.

Pat the food you're cooking dry with paper towels, using your fingers, rub the outside surface of the meat or fish with the seasoning blend. If you have time allow the food to stand at room temperature for 15 minutes before cooking.

cajun spice rub

Great for rubbing into the skin of roast chicken or for sprinkling on lamb chops. Try this rub for the Blackened Salmon Salad (page 76).

1 teaspoon dried oregano
1 teaspoon dried thyme
1 teaspoon garlic powder
1 teaspoon pimentón (Spanish oak-smoked paprika)
1 teaspoon cayenne pepper
1 teaspoon light brown sugar
1 teaspoon dry mustard powder
2 teaspoons sea salt flakes

In a bowl mix all the spices together and then store in a dry screw-top jar until required. To use, follow method for Mustard and Herb Rub (left).

middle eastern rub

This spicy seasoning works well with steak, lamb chops, pork fillet, or oily fish. It can also be rubbed onto chicken skin or a shoulder of lamb before roasting, which will give the meat an intense aromatic taste. For speed, I've given ground herbs here, but you can grind whole spices.

2 tablespoons extra virgin olive oil
½ teaspoon ground ginger
½ teaspoon ground coriander
½ teaspoon ground cumin
½ teaspoon sea salt
½ teaspoon cardamom pods, pods removed and seeds crushed
½ teaspoon ground cinnamon
½ teaspoon ground allspice
½ teaspoon cayenne pepper
finely grated zest of 1 orange

Mix the spice ingredients together in a bowl with the olive oil. To use, follow method for Mustard and Herb Rub (far left).

salad dressings

A good salad dressing is only as good as the ingredients you use. For simple salad leaves, drizzle extra virgin olive oil, add a drop of balsamic vinegar and a sprinkling of sea salt and freshly ground black pepper to a salad bowl before you add the salad leaves. Add a few sprigs of fresh green herbs, such as cilantro, basil, or mint, and you've got a masterpiece of a salad without any fuss.

blue cheese dressing

This is a great dressing for using up those leftover bits of blue cheese lurking in the back of your fridge. Blue cheese goes particularly well with pears or can be used to liven up a chicken salad. Once made, the dressing will keep for up to 1 week in the fridge.

2 oz. firm blue cheese, such as Stilton or Roquefort

2 tablespoons sherry or cider vinegar

3 tablespoons walnut or hazelnut oil

3 tablespoons safflower oil

1 teaspoon Worcestershire sauce

freshly squeezed lemon juice, to taste

freshly ground black pepper

Put all the ingredients, except the lemon juice, in the bowl of a food processor, process until smooth. Add a little lemon juice and pepper to taste.

caesar dressing

This is a speedy version of the popular dressing. Perfect with any green salad leaves and works well with roast chicken or avocado. Once made, the dressing will keep for up to 1 week in the fridge.

1 egg

1 garlic clove, crushed

2 teaspoons Worcestershire sauce

1 teaspoon anchovy essence

1 tablespoon freshly squeezed lime juice

3 tablespoons extra virgin olive oil

1 oz. Parmesan cheese, coarsely grated

freshly ground black pepper

Put the egg in a pan of cold water and bring to a boil. Boil for 1 minute and then plunge into cold water to stop the cooking process. Once the egg is cool enough to handle, crack it into a mini food processor and add the garlic, Worcestershire sauce, anchovy essence, lime juice, and olive oil. Process well, then stir in the Parmesan cheese and add pepper to taste.

sweet mustard dressing

This dressing is slightly sweeter than a classic vinaigrette. It has a creamy emulsified texture and is good for drizzling over sliced tomatoes and mozzarella and works well with bitter salad leaves like endive, arugula, or frisée lettuce. If you prefer, you could use yellow mustard instead of Dijon. Once made, the dressing will keep for up to 1 week in the fridge.

1 tablespoon Dijon mustard

2 teaspoons honey

1 tablespoon cider vinegar

6 tablespoons extra virgin olive oil

sea salt and freshly ground black pepper

Put all the ingredients in a screw-top jar and shake vigorously until the dressing is emulsified. Add salt and pepper to taste.

Other quick salad ideas:

★ **Instant Caesar Salad** Tear 1 head romaine lettuce into pieces and toss it in some Quick Caeser Dressing (see facing page). Add some store-bought croûtons and pre-cooked bacon pieces and grate some Parmesan cheese over the top.

★ **Quick Saffron Potato Salad** Mix 2 tablespoons of Garlic and Saffron Aioli (see below) with 8 oz. cooked new potatoes.

★ **Mixed Bean Salsa** Mix the Mediterranean Salsa (see below) with a drained can of mixed beans, 2 chopped plum tomatoes, and some chopped spinach and scallions.

★ **Quick Niçoise Salad** Mix the Herb Vinaigrette (see below left) with a can of tuna. Toss in some salad leaves, chopped cucumber, cherry tomatoes, sliced red onion, black olives, and hard-cooked eggs.

herb vinaigrette

The sprigs of herbs and garlic used here will infuse the vinaigrette the longer they are left in the dressing. It is the most useful and versatile dressing in my kitchen. Once made, the dressing will keep for up to 1 week in the fridge.

1 tablespoon freshly squeezed lemon juice

1 tablespoon white wine vinegar or tarragon vinegar

sea salt and freshly ground black pepper

1 teaspoon sugar

7 tablespoons extra virgin olive oil

1 garlic clove, halved

a few fresh herb sprigs, such as tarragon, cilantro, or mint

Put the lemon juice, vinegar, salt, and pepper to taste, sugar, and olive oil in a screw-top jar. Shake the jar vigorously until the dressing is smooth. Add the garlic halves and herb sprigs.

garlic and saffron aioli

This is delicious served with broiled or grilled fish or chicken, or it can be served as a dip for potato wedges. Once made, this dressing will keep for up to 1 week in the fridge.

⅔ cup good-quality mayonnaise

2 garlic cloves, crushed

a pinch of cayenne pepper

a pinch of saffron threads

1 tablespoon extra virgin olive oil

Put all the ingredients in a bowl and whisk until combined. Cover with plastic wrap and chill in the fridge for about 1–2 hours, to allow the saffron flavor to develop fully. Stir well before serving.

mediterranean salsa

This is perfect for cheering up broiled or grilled fish fillets or chicken breasts, or serving as a dip. A spoonful will also brighten up a canned soup. Once made, it will keep for up to 1 week in the fridge.

1 tablespoon red wine vinegar

2 tablespoons small capers, rinsed, drained, and finely chopped

1 garlic clove, crushed

½ teaspoon anchovy essence

½ teaspoon Dijon mustard

2 tablespoons chopped fresh herbs, such as basil, tarragon, parsley, and mint

freshly squeezed juice of ½ lemon

½ small onion, finely chopped

⅔ cup extra virgin olive oil

freshly ground black pepper

Put the vinegar, capers, garlic, anchovy essence, and mustard in a heavy-based bowl and use a sturdy wooden spoon to work the mixture until evenly combined. Whisk in the herbs, lemon juice, onion, olive oil, and pepper to taste.

index

conversion charts

Weights and measures have been rounded up or down slightly to make measuring easier.

Volume equivalents:

American	Metric	Imperial
1 teaspoon	5 ml	
1 tablespoon	15 ml	
¼ cup	60 ml	2 fl.oz.
⅓ cup	75 ml	2½ fl.oz.
½ cup	125 ml	4 fl.oz.
⅔ cup	150 ml	5 fl.oz. (¼ pint)
¾ cup	175 ml	6 fl.oz.
1 cup	250 ml	8 fl.oz.

Weight equivalents: **Measurements:**

Imperial	Metric	Inches	Cm
1 oz.	25 g	¼ inch	5 mm
2 oz.	50 g	½ inch	1 cm
3 oz.	75 g	¾ inch	1.5 cm
4 oz.	125 g	1 inch	2.5 cm
5 oz.	150 g	2 inches	5 cm
6 oz.	175 g	3 inches	7 cm
7 oz.	200 g	4 inches	10 cm
8 oz. (½ lb.)	250 g	5 inches	12 cm
9 oz.	275 g	6 inches	15 cm
10 oz.	300 g	7 inches	18 cm
11 oz.	325 g	8 inches	20 cm
12 oz.	375 g	9 inches	23 cm
13 oz.	400 g	10 inches	25 cm
14 oz.	425 g	11 inches	28 cm
15 oz.	475 g	12 inches	30 cm
16 oz. (1 lb.)	500 g		
2 lb.	1 kg		

Oven temperatures:

110°C	(225°F)	Gas ¼
120°C	(250°F)	Gas ½
140°C	(275°F)	Gas 1
150°C	(300°F)	Gas 2
160°C	(325°F)	Gas 3
180°C	(350°F)	Gas 4
190°C	(375°F)	Gas 5
200°C	(400°F)	Gas 6
220°C	(425°F)	Gas 7
230°C	(450°F)	Gas 8
240°C	(475°F)	Gas 9